Fix It in the Mix

In the early 70s, Paul Hornsby set the Southern music industry in Macon, Georgia, on its toes. A musical giant in his own right and stellar record producer for Capricorn, he brought the best out of artists who are now internationally known American icons. The work he produced has stood the test of time and are true American classics. Charlie Daniels, Marshall Tucker, and others applauded this man's work and friendship. A great read from the backwoods of Alabama to the inside story of Capricorn Records!
—Sandy "Blue Sky" Wabegijig, former wife of Dickey Betts and mother of Jessica

Paul Hornsby was my mentor in the days when I was a young musician looking for opportunities. If not for Paul, I would never have been able to have the career I've had. He is still my hero and one of my best friends—thanks, Paul!
—Chuck Leavell, musical director and keyboardist for the Rolling Stones and former member of The Allman Brothers Band

Fix it in the Mix has chronicled a fascinating story of Paul Hornsby's life as a musician and acclaimed record producer. From his early days as a musician, his time with brothers Duane and Gregg Allman and Johnny Sandlin in the Hour Glass band, and his tremendous success producing records for Charlie Daniels, The Marshall Tucker Band and others, and finally as an owner-operator of his own recording studio, Paul has a great story to tell. I have known him for many years, but after reading his new book, I feel I know him better.
—Willie Perkins, former road manager for The Allman Brothers Band and author of *No Saints, No Saviors*

Paul is my producer. He'll always be my producer. He produced all of the records our band did at Capricorn Records that are so special to me. I think the world of Paul and I am so glad his story has been written. It's a story that deserves to be told.
—Paul T. Riddle, original drummer for The Marshall Tucker Band

Eric Quincy Tate's time with Paul Hornsby was very short—one album, but everlasting. In the studio, Paul was like part of the band—he seemed to fit right in. I can't say anything that hasn't already been said about this guy. He is the complete package when it comes to Southern Rock, and this book tells the tale!
—David Cantonwine, bassist for the Eric Quincy Tate band

MUSIC AND THE
AMERICAN SOUTH

For a list of titles in the series, see the back of this book.

Fix It in the Mix

A Memoir

By Paul Hornsby

with Michael Buffalo Smith

MERCER UNIVERSITY PRESS
Macon, Georgia
2021

MUP/ P620

© 2021 by Mercer University Press
Published by Mercer University Press
1501 Mercer University Drive
Macon, Georgia 31207
All rights reserved

25 24 23 22 21   5 4 3 2 1

Books published by Mercer University Press are printed on acid-free paper that meets the requirements of the American National Standard for Information Sciences—Permanence of Paper for Printed Library Materials.

Printed and bound in the United States.

This book is set in Adobe Caslon Pro.

Cover/jacket design by Burt&Burt.

Library of Congress Cataloging-in-Publication Data
  Hornsby, Paul, author. | Smith, Michael Buffalo, author.
Fix it in the mix : a memoir / Paul Hornsby with Michael Buffalo Smith.
[1st.] | Macon : Mercer University Press, 2021. | Includes bibliographical references and index. | Identifiers: LCCN 2020050715 | ISBN 9780881467819
(paperback) Subjects: LCSH: Hornsby, Paul. | Sound recording executives
and producers—Southern States—Biography. | LCGFT: Autobiographies.
LCC ML429.H77 A3 2021 | DDC 781.66092—dc23 | LC record available
at https://lccn.loc.gov/2020050715

Contents

Foreword by Charlie Daniels   xi

Introduction by Michael Buffalo Smith   1

1. Beginnings   3

2. Rolling with the Tide   18

3. The Five Minutes   28

4. Like Sand through the Hour Glass   39

5. Under the Sign of Capricorn   57

6. Macon Magic   67

7. Searchin' for a Rainbow   81

8. Capricorn Rising   95

9. Volunteer Jam   108

10. Going Indie with the Long Haired
    Country Boy   110

11. The All-American Redneck Who
    Inspired Muscadine Studios   119

12. The Reunion: The Capricorn
    Rhythm Section   129

13. Indians   132

14. Cowboys   136

15. Red Hot   140

Epilogue   145

Afterword: A Dream Come True
    by Michael Buffalo Smith   146
Appendix: Select Discography   (following 152)
Selected Reading   153
Special Thanks   154
About the Authors   157
Index   159
Music in the American South Series   165

Dedicated to

the memory of Jeanne Lowry Hornsby

1944–2000

Foreword

I was looking for someone, someone special, a record producer, but not *just* a record producer. I wanted one who not only had knowledge and respect for the music we created but who also could gain the confidence of the musicians in the band and deliver the kind of album we knew we were capable of creating, but so far had eluded us.

I wanted the big sound, raw energy, and spontaneous style I was hearing on the Marshall Tucker records. I wanted to go to Capricorn Studios in Macon, Georgia, away from the glitter and glare of the "music business." New York hadn't worked, and Nashville was, at that time, set up for a single artist, accompanied by professional studio musicians, and not quite ready for guitar players who turned their amplifiers up till the speakers distorted and played ten-minute jams.

Paul Hornsby was the final piece of the puzzle, a road musician who had played keyboard with some of the most influential musicians the South had ever produced. He was studio savvy, lived in Macon, and, most important of all, was the guy who was making the Marshall Tucker Band sound like a runaway train.

A date was arranged, and we moved our gear into Capricorn Studios. Before we even got the first few tracks, I knew it was one of the best things I'd ever done.

Paul was everything the CDB needed. He could work with the engineers getting killer sounds; he could talk with the musicians about chord progressions and ideas to improve the parts they were playing; and, most important of all, he knew when we had delivered "the" performance.

Paul is the most laid back, unassuming, calm, cool, and understated character I ever worked with. When he said "that's decent" he was actually saying that we had just recorded an album-worthy take.

Our first project together was titled *Fire on the Mountain*. It was our first gold and subsequently multiplatinum album, a true milestone in our career, and Paul played an indispensable role in its success.

Paul is a friend, a man I both like and admire and a definite giant in the music that has come to be known as Southern Rock. He was there at its inception, shared the stage with Duane Allman, the guy who started it all, and he nurtured its growth and innovation through his influence with the Marshall Tucker Band, CDB, Wet Willie, and many others.

His work has stood the test of time, and some of the records he produced in those pioneering days are mainstays on classic radio.

I am so glad that the chief chronicler of the genre, Michael Buffalo Smith, has undertaken the telling of his story, the story of an Alabama country boy who played such a significant role in my early career.

Thanks, Paul.

Love and God bless,
—*Charlie Daniels*

Introduction

The music industry had never seen anything quite like Capricorn Records when it sprung to life in the sleepy little town of Macon, Georgia, back in 1969. Finally, there was a record label and studio complete with a built-in management company catering to the sounds of the South. Phil and Alan Walden had already enjoyed major success in R&B, managing acts like Percy Sledge, Sam and Dave, and the dynamic Otis Redding. Following the unexpected death of Otis, the Waldens regrouped, and with the blessings (and money) of Jerry Wexler from Atlantic Records, they founded Capricorn Records in Macon. The decade that followed was the heyday for the music that came to be called Southern rock, beginning with Duane Allman and the Allman Brothers band. The studio had two primary record producers, Johnny Sandlin and Paul Hornsby, although they often employed the iconic Tom Dowd as well. The hundreds of great records that sprung from that well were produced mostly by these two gentlemen, who were also top-flight musicians and played on many, many records.

With the success of Capricorn Records, almost every major record label began hiring Southern groups. Polydor had the Atlanta Rhythm Section, Epic had the Charlie Daniels Band, London signed ZZ Top, and MCA had Lynyrd Skynyrd. And those were just the beginning. One has to wonder how history would have looked upon all these bands had there never been a Phil Walden, Jerry Wexler, Frank Fenter, Johnny Sandlin, or, God help us, a Paul Hornsby. The truth is, it all started right there in little ol' Macon, Georgia.

"Southern rock" is hard to define because, rather than conform to a particular commercial sound, Walden and crew set about encouraging individuality. Southern rock is more about attitude than anything. It's the attitude that Duane Allman had, the same one Ronnie Van Zant and Tommy Caldwell in the Marshall Tucker band both had. It was never "How are we going to get over that mountain?"—it was "We are going through that mountain!" Phil Walden had that attitude on the business end. Frank Fenter had it on the entertainment end. And the group of producers, writers, and performers all had it in spades.

It was here that Southern rock was born, kicking and screaming in the streets after leaving Grant's Lounge at 2 a.m., or after a late breakfast with Mama Louise Hudson at the H&H Restaurant. This is the true story of a man without whom Southern rock may have never been born. A man who's been a hero of mine since I read the liner notes on the very first Marshall Tucker Band LP back in 1972. A man who is still producing today. A man I am now proud to call friend and whom I proudly proclaim as my own record producer all these years later. A true musical legend. Paul Hornsby.

—*Michael Buffalo Smith*
Spartanburg, South Carolina

2

1

Beginnings

My daddy, Marvin Edward Hornsby ("Ed"), was in the Army in World War II, and my mother, Magdalene Maddox Hornsby, was about ready to "rake straw," as they say. When a cow's getting ready to have a calf, they go to rakin' straw. Well, when she got ready to have me, she came home to her parents, my grandparents, Isaiah and Stella Maddox, outside of Elba, Alabama, out in what they call the "flats." That is out in the Pea River swamps—the river was originally named by the Creek Indians who were living in that area. If you look me up on the internet, it'll say "from Elba, Alabama." I was born there and stayed there a few days, so I guess you could say I was from the flats. I was raised on our farm, which was about fourteen miles from Elba, way out in the country, out around Pea River (but Pea River runs through all those places). The closest towns were New Brockton—six miles in one direction—and Enterprise—ten miles in the other direction.

My mother and father had both grown up in farming communities. That's what most everybody did back then. My mother was born and raised outside of Elba, and I was born in the same house that she was. That old house is still standing, but it's used to store hay bales now. I wish it could have been saved.

My daddy was a real cocky young gentleman. He was walking the streets of Elba one day and saw my mother. They caught each other's eyes then both turned to look back to see if the other was looking. Somehow, they eventually got together. Then I came along. I was their only child.

Our farm was only six miles from town, but it might as well have been six hundred. We didn't have any neighbors, and the people closest to where we lived were my grandparents who lived up the road. My grandparents pretty much raised me. My daddy would be out working the farm, and my mother took a job in town doing books for her brother's business, so once I got to school age, they recruited my grandparents, Ace and Bertie Hornsby, to take care of me after I'd get off the school bus.

We were living near poverty, I guess. Of course, I didn't know what poverty was back then—I just thought everybody lived that way. At Christmas, there wasn't a Santa Claus in every store like there is now. There was just one, like there's just one Jesus Christ, so Santa Claus was right up there in biblical proportions. I can remember listening to the radio when I was just a little ol' bitty boy, about five. The announcer came on and said that Santa Claus himself was going to make an appearance in Enterprise that afternoon, and he'd be flying in on a helicopter. Helicopters were easier to find in our area than reindeer. When I heard the announcement, I took off running out the back door to the barn where

4

my Daddy was working. When I got there, I was so out of breath I couldn't talk. Daddy thought the house was on fire. I was stuttering and trying to speak. I finally got the words out, "Santa Claus is coming to Enterprise in a helicopter! If we hurry, we can get down there before he leaves!" I just knew that my Daddy was going to stop what he was doing and rush us down there. I couldn't believe when he wasn't as impressed by this Santa Claus business as I was. He said, "Son, I can't drop everything to go down and see Santa Claus. I have several more hours of work to do before nightfall." It took me years to get over that. So, I didn't get to see Santa Claus until years later, and by then it didn't matter.

There's one story from my childhood on the farm that I have never lived down. If I go to a family reunion, the older people kid me about it. Like a lot of people my age where I came from, we didn't have indoor bathrooms until I was about seven years old. We had an outhouse, and I dreaded the cold weather. To use the bathroom, I'd have to go outside, pull out my privates, and let that cold wind hit me. Well, we also had a covered porch, and the floor had cracks in it, so my five-year-old brain came up with the perfect solution. To keep from going to the outhouse, I'd lie on the floor, stick my privates through that crack, and let it fly under the house. I got to where I enjoyed it, and I didn't have to use that outhouse as much.

That might have been the end of the story, but Mama kept these chickens, Rhode Island Reds. One day, one of those chickens came along and saw that little thing hanging down between the cracks in the porch floor. You can imagine what happened. Afterward, I told my parents about it. There were a lot of foxes in the area too, so they kidded me that I'd been bitten by a mad fox. Of course, I knew it was a chicken because I saw it when it let go and ran away. For many years after that, they joked and asked me if I'd been bitten by a mad fox lately. It's a wonder that I ever fathered any children after that.

I never was cut out for farm labor. I did pick some cotton, but I remember how I loved lying on the linoleum in the house. We didn't have air conditioning, and that linoleum was cold in the summertime. It felt good. I had a fan blowing on me, and I'd lie there in my short pants, barefoot with no shirt on, and read my comic books. I loved reading comic books. Once in a while, my daddy would get onto me and tell me I wasn't going to amount to anything just reading those comics, but they were teaching me to read. He'd say, "I'm gonna teach you a trade." I don't know how many times I heard that. Then he'd put me on some farm task that I hated. I'd look around, and when he got preoccupied with something else, I'd slip away, back to my comic books.

He always had cattle, but one year he decided to raise hogs. I don't ever want anything to do with swine. They are hard to keep up, and we had to repair the fence daily where they broke it. At that time, there were what was called screw worms. In South America, they were called a bot fly. If you were on an expedition down there and got cut or scratched, a bot fly could land on you and lay eggs in the cut. The larvae are like maggots, but where maggots eat only rotted flesh, bot flies will eat good, healthy flesh. Those screw worms will eat you up. I don't know if that's what we had in Alabama or not, but, if you had livestock, you had to constantly watch them for cuts from barbed wire or whatever, or else you might look over and see a huge sore being eaten up by screw worms. I've seen my daddy with a pair of tweezers pulling those things off cows and hogs one at a time, and he'd slap some tar on the sores to keep more screw worm flies from landing on it.

One day he grabbed me and took me outside. He told me he was going to teach me a "trade." He had me hold the tar jar, and it had a wooden paddle in it. I held that jar in my right hand, and a bucket in my left hand. I hadn't caught on to what was happening yet; I just knew it was part of my "trade." I was just a little ol' boy too. He had a well-sharpened pocketknife. He didn't want these boar hogs to crossbreed with his other hogs, so he'd catch one of those little half-grown pigs between his legs with the tail end sticking out in front. Then he'd reach down, cut off its balls, and toss them in the bucket I was holding. Then he'd slap some of that tar on the cut, and that pig would be squealing for dear life. That pig was dismissed and went off squealing and he was on to the next one. We had a bunch of them. All I could think of while holding the ball bucket quickly filling up was wondering if this was going to be my "trade."

Before we had electricity, we had oil lamps (Aladdin was the brand name) we used for light at night. If you had a shortage of them, you'd carry one from room to room. If you'd never experienced anything else, then that was all you knew. I remember when we finally got electricity. After the man who was wiring the house left, I ran around and turned on every light in the house, and when my mother got home, I told her I did it so she could see to get in. I thought she'd be proud of me. She told me that we don't turn them on unless we have to, and that was my first lesson in conserving electricity.

Daddy was well known locally in those days as a musician. I always say it's a miracle I didn't end up in country music because I have an Uncle Willie, an Uncle Waylon, and an Aunt Merle. If I'd had a Hank in there, I would have been a shoo-in. My Uncle Willie told me how my daddy, Ed, had been an old-time fiddle player since he was a teenager, but they didn't have honky-tonks or local places like that to per- form in back then. It was Prohibition, and the whole country was dry. In fact, Coffee County remained dry until a few years ago. The only places Daddy could play were house par- ties, square dances, and cake walks. Many times after I had grown up, I'd be riding in the truck with my daddy, and he'd nearly run us off the road, pointing to a chimney out away from the road, and he'd say, "I played a dance there back in 1931." He'd always have some sort of a story attached to it. Uncle Willie said, "Back in those days when your daddy would play the fiddle, he'd have women all over him." I said, "Yeah. That's the musician's life. That's why we do what we do."

Thinking back, I was exposed to music before I was even born. Aside from my daddy's playing "old time" fiddle (not to be confused with bluegrass), my earliest musical influence was my dad's cousin, James Tindol. The tunes Daddy learned, he learned from other old-time fiddlers, and they learned 'em from *other* old-time fiddlers. A lot of those songs probably came over from the old country, from Europe, you know, from England, Ireland. Old time music. It was almost an insult to my daddy to be referred to as a bluegrass musician because—it's funny—he had his own way of doing things and thinking about things. Bluegrass has those high, lonesome vocals, the Bill Monroe vocals, where you sing up high. Daddy didn't think that was manly. He thought a man ought to sing down low, so he didn't want to be involved with bluegrass music.

He and his cousins, the Tindols, used to play schoolhouses, house parties, fundraisers, and all kind of stuff. Those were the only money-making draws in the area. They'd always pass the hat, and if they got a quarter for a gallon of gas to get home, they felt like they had a good night. At least it didn't cost them to play. They never made any money and played just for the sheer joy of playing. Daddy never grasped the idea that you could make a living playing music. I've doubted it a few times myself. Some of my earliest musical memories are of being dragged around and watching him and James play for square dances or of being a punk kid, running around getting into trouble while he was on stage fiddling.

I was quiet and shy as a kid. I attended New Brockton Elementary School/New Brockton High School where all twelve grades were in the same building, with elementary on one wing and high school on the other. Back when I was in high school, the town population was probably around 1,500 people, and there may be less than that now. When farming kind of went out of style, the younger people took jobs outside of town. The town began to dwindle, and then the railroad closed. I remember when they pulled the tracks up. But it used to be a thriving little town. The only two people who made a name for themselves in the music business out of New Brockton were me and Don Helms, who was the original steel guitar player for Hank Williams, Sr. His dad worked across the street from where my mom worked.

When I was eight years old, my mother had an old upright piano she had bought for seventy-five bucks. Seventy-five bucks was a big chunk of money anywhere back then, and, being the kind of slacker that I was, I hated school, I hated studying, and I hated all that stuff. In about the third grade, I'd see this little girl get to leave class early. I found out where she was going: to piano lessons. I thought, "Huh…boy, I'd like to do that. I'd like to be able to get out of this class." I convinced my mother that I wanted to take piano lessons, so she bought this seventy-five-dollar piano. About the first or second lesson I took, I thought, "Oh my God, this is the worst thing I've ever had to do in my life! I don't think I like it. I don't want to do this—I'd rather be back doing arithmetic." But she'd already spent her seventy-five bucks, she'd already made that investment in me, and, by God, I was going to learn to play piano. I was stubborn, but I went to piano lessons a few years. Of course, they never let you play the stuff you wanted to play. It was always that

10

old corny shit out of a book, and if you tried to play it your way, they hit you on your knuckles with a ruler or something, you know. Every piano teacher I ever had did that, and I just hated it. I ended up quitting, and I was music-less for a few years. So, it's a wonder that I ever became a piano player in years following.

Daddy bought a reel-to-reel tape recorder when I was twelve years old. It was a Pentron. It was monaural and had one little cheap microphone with it. I started recording everything on that little machine. When I turned fourteen, I was thrilled to record myself playing guitar and then hearing it back. I'm sure that was the seed that grew into my love for engineering, mixing, and producing.

If it hadn't been for my dad, I probably would have never played any music. My daddy had seen that I wanted to be a guitar player, so he brought home two guitars one time when I was fourteen. The guy he got them from said I could try them both out, and he'd sell either one for fifteen dollars. One was a shiny red Silvertone acoustic guitar, almost new, and the other was a Gibson jumbo hollow body. I didn't know anything about guitars, but I was immediately riveted to that red Silvertone. Daddy struck a few chords on it. Then he struck a chord on the Gibson and said, "Just listen to that tone!" "Yeah, Daddy," I said, "but that other one is red!" Luckily, he knew more about guitars than I did, so he bought the Gibson. That guitar had been well played before Daddy got ahold of it, and I always wondered who had owned it before. It wasn't a cheap guitar; it was probably top of the line for its time. But what I remember was the way it smelled back then. I thought, "Now that's the way music smells." It's funny, it had those old, tarnished Black Diamond strings on it. They just had a smell to 'em.

My daddy showed me a few chords on the guitar. He could play some guitar as well as fiddle, and most of the tunes he played didn't have more than three chords anyway, so I soon mastered those three chords. I could play along on any tunes he knew, and within six months, I knew more guitar than he did. Then I got exposed to Chet Atkins's guitar playing, and that changed my life. Soon after that I heard the Ventures. The first time I heard a twanger-bar, it was on a Ventures record. That was the most wonderful sound I'd ever heard. I heard "Walk Don't Run." I heard that twanger-bar...man, I wish music could sound that good to me again! Everything was brand new.

At that age, I was a loner in school. There, a lot of kids were from town, so I felt different from them, and them from me. I never stood out in anything and pretty much always sat in the back seat on the back row and hoped the teacher wouldn't call on me. We had assembly—I can't remember if it was weekly or once a month—but one day there was a boy who was older than me, and he was sitting up on-stage during an assembly and picking an acoustic guitar, playing "Wildwood Flower." The girls all had their eyes right on him. I thought that must be something special right there. I'd give anything if I could play like that. When I got a little older, Daddy taught me to play "Wildwood Flower," just open chords because he didn't play any barre chords whatsoever.

Between that Gibson guitar and hearing "Wildwood Flower," my mind stayed on music. I remember sitting in the back row in high school and while the teacher was talking, I was there doodling in my books, drawing guitars. If you went back and looked at my old schoolbooks, you'd find guitars drawn all over them. While the other boys were sneaking and looking at *Playboy* magazines, I was designing guitars, and all the guitars I drew had Bigsby tailpieces on them. I thought that was the coolest thing in the world, but I never owned a guitar with a Bigsby until about five years ago. I thought, before I die, I've got to own a guitar with a Bigsby on it, so I bought an Epiphone jazz guitar with a Bigsby. The tailpiece and the tuning keys are gold-plated. The first Bigsbys I ever saw were on Gretsch guitars, like the Chet Atkins–type guitars. Then the Ventures came along, using that whammy bar to dive bomb those chords on "Walk Don't Run" and songs like that. Between the Ventures and Chet Atkins, you didn't really need anybody else.

Once I learned to play that Gibson—this would have been in the late '50s—I kind of moved on past old-time fiddle favorites. There was nowhere to play and nobody to play with, and the only other person I knew of at that time that even owned an electric guitar was a schoolmate of mine who was about two years older. His name was Wendell Bell. He lived in the county adjoining ours, and I used to drive to his house just to look at the electric guitar before I ever learned to play it. He could play the heck out of it. I just thought, "God, that's a wonderful thing right there." He still plays today. I talk to Wendell every few years just to tell him what a fan I was of his growing up. I thought he was the best guitar player in the world back then. I remember him having a band, and they were out of my league. They were seniors and I was just a kid in the ninth grade, but I really wanted to hang out with them and play with them. Of course, they didn't have time for this kid; they had to go play music for the girls. I'd see him playing those 9th chords up and down the neck of the guitar, and I'd think, "God, if I could only do that!"

His guitar was a Fender, the first Fender guitar I ever saw. It was a Fender Music Master, and it cost around $119. It had one pickup on it. The Duo Sonic, which was about $150, was the same guitar, but it had two pickups. I don't ever see any of those Music Masters around nowadays. I see plenty of Telecasters and Strats, but never any Music Masters. These were almost like a three-quarter size guitar. They were a little smaller than Strats and Telecasters. It had all the tuning pegs on one side, and I thought that was cool. I had to have one. It took me about a year of playing on an old Silvertone that had strings about two inches high off the fret board. If you learn to play on one of those guitars, you knew you were committed because you would be nearly crippled for life playing these things. Permanent dents in your fingertips. But I finally got a Fender Music Master just like my friend had. People would just come and gawk at that thing because there just weren't any around. The area of the country I was from wasn't musical at all. Somebody might have an old Sears and Roebuck guitar like I started on that they played on the back porch, but that was about it.

Opportunities to play music were slim to none where I lived back then. I was always extremely shy—I reckon I still am. I was sitting around one time; I think I had learned two chords on this guitar. I was playing those two chords and a girl walked over and talked to me! That changed my life. It only took two chords and a girl talked to me and I thought, "Huh, I see what I got. I see the route I need to take from now on."

At sixteen, I went to my first rock 'n' roll concert at the Houston County Farm Center in Dothan. It was Roy Orbison. The show also featured Bruce Channel of "Hey Baby" fame and a local band, the Webbs, who joined Orbison and became the Candymen. That just set me on fire. I thought, "I have to do this."

Music was magical back in those days. Most of the time it cost me to play, but I didn't mind. The first time I ever got paid to play, that is, money I could keep and put in my pocket and leave with, was at a dance. There was a group called the Goodson Brothers, and they had a dance at the National Guard Armory, which was up the road in the next county. (This was at a time when the Armory was one of the few places to play.) One of the brothers was in the National Guard and had to go off to summer camp, and they asked me to fill in. I'm sure they had never heard me play before, but they had just heard that I played and that I owned a guitar. I played that Saturday night and made fifteen dollars. I had hit the higher pay scale, because fifteen dollars in 1960 was a pile of money. After that I knew without a doubt what my future held for me.

I still have the Gibson my daddy bought when I was fourteen. It's what's known as a Banner Gibson, because there's a banner across the headstock that reads, "Only a Gibson is Good Enough." It was made during the war years, 1943–1945. Gibson was supposed to be closed and making government war stuff; there's a book out about it called *Kalamazoo Gals* about the women who worked in the factory while the men were shipped off to the war. So, the women were making nonmusical products for the government, but they made these Banner Gibson guitars, and they are a pretty rare item these days. They were made for only three years, and they were made without a bar through the neck, unfortunately. They were also called a Southern Jumbo. Mine doesn't have a serial number because the paper decal that used to be on the inside is gone, but my daddy wrote his name in there with a pencil. That guitar stood in the corner of our house and was the only guitar in the house for years. About ten years ago, after my mother and daddy were gone, I decided to bring that guitar to town and put it in a place where there's a burglar alarm, and I still have that thing at the studio.

The more years that pass, the more I think that "old" is cool. Somebody, bless their heart, came up with the term "vintage." I like that—that and "retro." I remember the first studio ad I put in the Yellow Pages where I changed it from "lots of old instruments provided" to "lots of vintage instruments provided." It sounded much better. That vintage Gibson made its first appearance on a record just a few years ago.

Tommy Talton played some slide on it on a Lisa Biales album. It sounded like a million-dollar instrument.

2

Rolling with the Tide

I went to the University of Alabama when I got out of high school, and the world opened up. It was probably a mistake taking my guitar and amplifier with me when I went off to college; otherwise I may have gotten a degree in something. Instead, I majored in nightclubbing and kept the wee hours playing honky-tonks. I slept through some of the best classes the University of Alabama had to offer. I put in a year up there, but college wasn't my thing.

The first band I had was called the Barons. I had no idea what a band was supposed to be like. Before that, somebody might come by our house and they might have a guitar in their car, and we'd sit down and pick. There was no formality to it. I probably should have read more textbooks, but I had been bitten by the music bug and that's all I wanted to do.

There was this guy named Johnny Haas who was my best friend in college. He didn't know but about three chords. I told him not to worry about chords, I'd make him our bass player. We just had him use the four lower strings on the guitar and set the tone low on the amp. He had one of those Silvertone amps that is built into the guitar case, which was essentially useless. My amp was a pretty good size, so we both plugged into it. Then we had another boy, Chuck Beavers, who had a guitar, and he plugged into my amp too. All three of us were plugged into my amp. And our drummer John Gunder's "kit" consisted of a snare and a high hat. That was it. Looking back on our limited resources, it's amazing that we were able to play a reasonable facsimile of "Walk Don't Run" and all of the Ventures' greatest hits.

Then we started going to fraternity parties. I didn't even know at that point what a fraternity was, but we started crashing them and started seeing all these blues bands. People like Slim Harpo, or maybe Johnny Jenkins would come up from Macon with the Pinetoppers. I can't remember if Otis Redding was playing with them during that time or not. I started asking around how these bands got to play the fraternity parties. Someone said, "They audition." I didn't even know what that meant, so they explained that you come and play a sample of your music for free—and if they like you, they book your band. One day we took our mediocre equipment and went walking down University Avenue, ringing doorbells at these fraternity houses. At one house, this guy came out and asked what we wanted, and I told him we wanted to audition. So, he took us down to the basement where the party room was. We plugged up and started playing some Ventures song. We didn't get very far into it before he stopped us and said something to the effect of "Don't call us, we'll call you." Well, I took that as encouragement! We walked out the front door, and I said, "He said he was going to call us!" Johnny Haas was from New York, and he'd been around more than me, so he said, "No man, that ain't what he meant." He told me it was just an expression, and we'd never hear from them again.

We went on down to another house, and again we were invited to set up in the basement, and we started playing. The guy said, "You know, we are going to be having a party here in about three weeks. Would you play for sixty dollars?" I found out that was not per man, but for the whole band. But I would have paid *him*. Then he looked at our drummer's "kit," with that snare and high hat, and asked, "Don't you have a bass drum?" He said, "You know, a bass drum just adds so much to your music. We might be able to locate one by the time of the party. If we get you one will you play it?" The drummer was like "Yeah, sure! I'll play it."

Three weeks later party night arrived. The guy told us he couldn't get a bass drum, but he got us a floor tom-tom. "Can you play that?" he asked. Our drummer said he could, so they set up the drum, and every time that guy looked over at our drummer, he'd reach over and hit that tom. It didn't matter where we were in the song, he'd hit that drum. We were on our way!

We had some business cards printed up. A couple of us lived in the dorm where there was one pay phone, so we put that number on the business card. The dorm was about four stories high, and the pay phone was on the bottom floor. There was a man who stayed on the bottom floor, like a den mother, to keep law and order. I think we got one call from the card, and the den father answered and went over to the stairwell and yelled up, "Anybody here know the Barons?

20

Some guy wants to speak to the Barons." I went running down those stairs as fast as I could. That was the beginning of my band days in college.

There were bands everywhere, there were musicians, there were people playing, and there was music. That was also when I was first exposed to Black musicians. I don't think I'd ever seen a Black musician before. And there were these blues bands and people like Slim Harpo and Arthur Alexander, a lot of the people who had started out in Muscle Shoals. At the time, I didn't know a thing about Muscle Shoals, so I was exposed to a lot of different stuff. I was considered a pretty hot, flashy guitar player by that time. I remember auditioning for a band and playing every lick I knew. Then they asked if I knew any Chuck Berry. I said, "Who's Chuck Berry?" They said, "Can't you play 'Johnny B. Goode'?" and I said "Man, I never heard that in my life!" That band still hired me.

After spending most of my freshman year sleeping through classes during the day and honky-tonk guitar picking at night, I made the Dean's List...the list of people to be *sent home*. I went right home after my freshman year when my parents ended my subsidy, and I was put to work at my dad's welding shop back in New Brockton, Alabama. It looked like I was faced with either donning a welding mask or pulling a six-foot drag sack along a row of Pea River cotton. Neither appealed to me.

Then, one day at the welding shop, the phone rang. I received the call from either Fred Styles or Doug Hogue, I forget which. They wanted to know if I would be interested in coming back up to Tuscaloosa to audition for the Pacers band. I think I left before sundown. I packed enough clothes to stay because I was confident I'd pass the audition. After all, I knew the complete Ventures repertoire. My parents showed their concern about what I would live on. Well, to my nineteen-year old way of thinking, if I could just eat once a month, I could survive. Either because of my Ventures knowledge or in spite of it, I passed the audition. I was the guitar player for the Pacers. Turns out we ate at least twice a month. I was the skinniest guitar player in Tuscaloosa for a while, but who needs to eat when they can play music? The Pacers turned into a progression of bands I was a part of over the next few years.

Eventually, though, everybody has to eat. Luckily, I had a friend named Bob Cunningham who was a guitar player. I knew that he taught guitar lessons at a local music store. One night he called me and asked if I would like to take over teaching his guitar students. I told him I wasn't sure I could do that because he had taught them how to read music, and I couldn't read a note. "You can do it," he said. "You just have to stay a page or two ahead of your students. You can learn it." What's more, he wanted me to start the next afternoon. I thought he was kidding. But then I thought about it; if I could just make enough to get by, I wouldn't have to go to work in the cotton fields of South Alabama. I went out and bought a couple of guitar books, started practicing, and learned to read music that night. I wasn't yet good enough though and got to wondering what would happen if they asked me to play. So, I bandaged up my hand and told them

I couldn't play for a couple of days because I had gotten my hand slammed in the car door. That bought me another day or two, and when the third day rolled around, I had it down. I was playing some good stuff. So, I was able to stay out of the cotton patch. Before I knew it, I had more than eighty students and was doing well. I bought myself a color TV on credit. I had one of the first color TVs in Tuscaloosa from teaching guitar lessons. It only cost twenty-eight dollars a month. Only one show came on in color at the time—*Voyage to the Bottom of the Sea*. It came on Sunday nights at 6:30. I had a friend named Bill Connell, who later played with the Allman Joys. He used to come over on Sunday nights to watch that show with me. It was a big deal.

I taught guitar lessons for about seven months, and then we took a break for the summer to go and play in Pensacola with the Five Minutes. When I came back from Florida after three months, I had to go looking for a job again. I went to work at the Tuscaloosa Music Service. I now had a wife and was having to start all over and was worrying about starving. The owner, Cliff Hurter, gave me a job and the key to the store, and told me to come and open up every morning at eight o'clock. He would come in around noon and take over. He told me that after school was out for the day, I could teach guitar lessons in the store. So, for that half a day in the store he paid me twenty dollars for five days work and lessons. After withholding, I got to take home eighteen whole dollars to support myself and my wife! One of the first fights my wife and I had was when she took that eighteen dollars and went and bought a week's worth of groceries with it. I just had a fit. I looked in the refrigerator and said, "Hell! You didn't even get any beer!"

With eighty-eight students a week, I brought a lot of business into that store. That's a lot of traffic. They would come in and buy strings and picks or guitars. That benefited the store and benefited me too. But that was 1964, and I taught there until fall 1966. Then I went on the road with The Five Minutes followed by the Hour Glass. After all of that was over, Cliff was kind enough to give me my job back, and I worked there for another nine months before moving to Macon. That was the last time I ever gave guitar lessons.

Around 1965, I branched out and started playing organ and then piano after hearing Eric Burdon and the Animals. Alan Price, with his portable Vox organ, impressed me a lot. I thought that keyboard was the coolest thing I'd ever seen. The Five Minutes were already playing "House of the Risin' Sun," and I thought if I had one of those organs, I could play it, and we'd be authentic when we played that tune. Before long, I bought a Farfisa Combo Compact organ, which was the next thing to a Vox. I remember that I got it on Monday and played my first gig with it on Friday.

That became the standard piece of gear in bands back then. That was well before digital instruments had appeared. In the best-equipped bands around, the standard keyboard rig was a Wurlitzer electric piano with a Farfisa organ sitting on top. With this set-up, you could play "What'd I Say" by Ray Charles and "House of the Risin' Sun" by the Animals, and you'd be unstoppable. I played the hell out of that thing and got everything I could get out of it for six months. Then,

I came across a Jimmy Smith record and the Hammond organ. That changed my life! That was real organ playing, and a Farfisa was never gonna cut it. I had to have one right away. Up until this time, I had been playing guitar, then adding the Hammond, I continued to play them both through the end of the Five Minutes, right on through the Hour Glass days. Throughout my band days I was playing guitar and keyboards.

I bought my first Hammond about 1966 and had it cut down to make it portable. We had a local electronics guy, George Winters, who fixed all the amps and equipment for the bands around town. I bought this organ, and I said, "George, I want you to take this organ, saw it in half, take the speakers off at the bottom—I don't need speakers—and take the amplifier out of it and put it in a separate little box and put me some legs on this thing so I can make it portable."

"Oh, man, no!" he said. "I can't take this beautiful instrument and cut it."

"Yeah, you can," I replied. "I know you can do it." I told him I wanted it where I could fold it up and put it in the trunk of a car. He thought I was nuts, but he did it. He put some sewing machine legs on the bottom of that thing, and I wound up playing that throughout the remaining year of the Five Minutes and got a Leslie tone cabinet I still use daily in my studio, Muscadine. I bought that thing new in 1966, and it still sounds wonderful. I had a good reason for making the organ portable—I don't know any old organ player to this day who doesn't have back problems, me included, from carrying those things.

I had just met Duane and Gregg Allman during the summer of '65 in Mobile. Then, they came and played at the University of Alabama with the Allman Joys. It was like the Beatles were coming when they showed up. Gregg was playing a portable Vox organ. I told him about my Hammond and that he really should get one. He and Duane came over to my house, and I showed him my Hammond and hit a few licks on it. He got excited and said, "show me that lick again!" He played it and said, "Man, I've got to have one of these." When we later joined forces in the Hour Glass, he played mine. We had also bought a Wurlitzer electric piano. We set them side by side; he'd play organ, and I'd play piano and vice-versa. I played guitar too. But that's how Gregg started playing a Hammond. As soon as the Hour Glass broke up, he bought his own. I listened to a lot of Jimmy Smith and Booker T. Jones. It was several years later that I really tried to be a piano player and there really is a difference. There's much more involved than just having similar keys. Organ playing has more to do with sounds. There's an art to working the drawbars and the fast/slow Leslie switch. My piano influences were Ray Charles and Dr. John. Back when I was a guitar player in the early '60s, every piano player I saw played Ray Charles stuff. There was not a great body of rock and roll piano music at the time; Ray was pretty much it. Every fraternity party I'd play, I'd have to play "What'd I Say." It was a standard, and your band had to play it whether you had a piano player or not. What Ray was playing defined rock and roll piano playing for me. Everybody wanted to play like Ray.

Then, when I started hearing Dr. John, his music was not that far from Ray Charles. Even though Ray came up in South Georgia and North Florida, it still had a lot of New Orleans flavor. Of course, Dr. John had his own influences in James Booker and Professor Longhair.

I think Mac Rebennack—better known by his stage name Dr. John—was the greatest piano player in the world. That's a lot of territory, I know. I had the pleasure of playing B-3 behind him for a while in the early 70s. That was a paid scholarship in a sense for me. That really lit a fire under me where piano playing was concerned. I'd be sitting behind the B-3 on stage and at the same time looking over his shoulder trying to see what he was doing. I think anyone who hears my playing will notice his influence on me. Chuck Leavell also played with Mac for a while. Mac left his mark on him as well.

3

The Five Minutes

I had I joined the Pacers in 1964. They had been around for a couple of years even before I joined them. We got an offer to go down and play in Florida for the summer, so those of us who were old enough quit our jobs and left everything to go down. We played one gig before going to Florida. It was in Gadsden, Alabama. After the gig, the sax player quit. Then the drummer. The group fell apart at the last minute, just as we had given up our day jobs. Out of desperation, Fred Styles, Paul Ballenger, and I drove up to Muscle Shoals to look for a drummer and sax player to take to Florida. I was on guitar then, Fred Styles was on bass, and Paul Ballenger was on piano and vocals. We couldn't find anybody in the Shoals who was willing to just take off and go with us. Then we got a lead on a sax player named Charlie Campbell who was down in Decatur, Alabama. He had played in a band called the Mark Five with Dan Penn and some of them. We called him, and he was interested in meeting us (making a long-distance call back then was a big deal, and you had to stand there feeding quarters into a pay phone). So, we drove down from Muscle Shoals to Decatur. When we mentioned needing a drummer, he told us about Johnny Sandlin, who also lived in Decatur. Anyhow, we all got together, "woodshedded" a few days, and struck out for Panama City—without any gig prospects or anything. The place we were supposed to audition with the original group had already filled the bill for the summer.

We started barn storming, knocking on doors and asking if we could play. We came across this woman who had a hole-in-the-wall, run-down bar. She said she'd never had a band there before, so we told her that if she'd let us play, we would just play for the door. So, we did. We made just a few dollars for gas. She asked us what the name of the band was, and we hadn't even had time to think of one. We told her if she'd give us about "five minutes" we'd come up with a name. So, we became the Five Minutes. I thought that sucked, but it would get us through the night and then we would think up a cooler name later. Of course, we never did. We had exhausted Panama City, so we went over to Pensacola. To make a long story short, we got a job playing at the Pensacola Beach Casino for the summer. It was a big beach amusement park—with a bar, game room, restaurant, snack bar, pinball machines, and dressing rooms for the beach. They agreed to let us play that first night, and they liked us and hired us on the spot. We played four nights a week in the lounge for the adult drinkers, and on Sunday afternoon we played in the ballroom for the teenagers. By the end of the summer, we were packing that place out. There were hundreds of teenagers who came out for the Sunday afternoon shows. We were promoting ourselves and buying radio airtime. It went great.

We returned to Tuscaloosa that fall and played college fraternities and parties. We became one of the most popular and best liked bands at the University of Alabama. We were tight, having played five nights a week in Pensacola.

The Five Minutes all had nicknames, and we teased each other endlessly. You would have thought we hated one another, but it was just us having fun. Johnny Sandlin was usually the one who started it. Johnny tended to be a little overweight, so we called him "Baby Huey" after the heavy duck in the cartoons, and over time it was shortened to "The Duck"; Charlie "The Lip" Campbell played sax (the name started out as "The Lying Lip" because we would catch him in lies all the time); Fred "The Pooh" Styles played bass (girls would call him all the time because they had nothing to do, and one of them called him "Hoggy Pooh," which we shortened to "The Pooh"); Paul "The Old Man" Ballenger (he was about five years older than us) played keys/vocal; Eddie Hinton was "The Bear"; and my name was "BB Berry" because of my playing guitar BB King and Chuck Berry licks. Eventually, the BB was dropped, and I became "The Berry," which lasted until Berry Oakley came on the scene. The Five Minutes sax player, Charlie Campbell, would later become an airline pilot. In 1993, he was flying the Hooter's plane carrying race car driver Alan Kulwicki when it crashed, killing everyone on board.

I remember that besides giving guitar lessons at that time, I occasionally offered keyboard lessons if I felt someone had the desire and talent to play. Chuck Leavell, a junior in high school, was several years younger than me and had a little band in town called the Misfitz. One day I asked him if he'd like keyboard lessons. He politely declined. I was just sure he was making a big mistake, but he seems to have done pretty well anyway.

The following summer (1965), we decided to go back to Pensacola. We added Eddie Hinton on guitar and vocals. I think Paul Ballenger dropped out at that time. After the summer, Charlie Campbell and Johnny Sandlin left. Bill Connell joined us on drums. We were then a four-piece group, which we continued to be until the end. I guess you'd say we were the four "Five Minutes." We kept getting asked where the fifth member was, and clubs didn't want to pay if they thought there was a member missing. Soon after, we just became the Minutes. Somewhere along the line, we came up with the spelling "the Men-Its."

In a bit of irony, our set list at the time included future Allman Brothers Band staples, "Stormy Monday," "Dimples," and "Turn on Your Love Light." Hinton and I started experimenting, playing around with some dual guitar parts, twin leads, and sometimes in harmony. I felt we were onto something with this style and we had more success with this band lineup than the ones before. Hinton became pretty renowned after he died, which is the way it usually goes. This was a few years before the formation of the Allman Brothers, when Duane and Dickey carried that idea to the moon.

I also played occasional sessions in Muscle Shoals early on. The Five Minutes recorded a single up there at FAME (Florence Alabama Music Enterprises) Studios in 1964 called "The Old Man" that got a lot of airplay in the college towns. We were engineered by the late, great Jimmy Johnson, who later became one of the Swampers. Before the Swampers, FAME had a studio band with Jerry Carrigan, David Briggs, and Norbert Putnam; they later became Elvis Presley's band. But that was pretty much the beginning of my studio work. Also, I would do occasional studio work at a studio called Boutwell's in Birmingham.

Thinking about the original FAME band...they had just made their move to Nashville and were becoming much sought-after session players. There was a time when my band, now called the 5 Men-Its, was booked for a gig in Huntsville, and two of our guys couldn't make it. We contacted Jerry Carrigan, and he and David Briggs filled in with us that night. "I like the way you play guitar," Briggs told me. "You could be a session player." He said, "If you can come up to Nashville this Saturday, I can get you on a Perry Como session." I had just turned twenty years old—he might as well have said it was Lawrence Welk. I was still waiting on a call from the Beatles! I was grateful that he thought of me and wondered many times over the years, "what if?" How different would my career have been if I'd started playing Perry Como sessions? Of course, Briggs and Carrigan went on to do even greater things.

At the time, Lonnie Mack was my first "guitar God." I had seen him play at the National Guard Armory in Birmingham, playing that Gibson Flying-V. That was just way too cool. His bass player had a bass that was painted blue. I had never seen one painted like that. The first thing I did was to take my sunburst Fender Jaguar to the body shop, have it stripped and painted blue.

The next summer (1966), Bill Connell left to join the Allman Joys, and Johnny Sandlin came back. We went back to Pensacola Beach and played at the Spanish Village. That fall, Fred Styles was two steps ahead of the draft, so he had to go back and stay in school. We hired Mabron "Wolf" McKinney on bass.

In September 1966, the Men-Its decided to go on "the road" and play music full-time. Our friends the Allman Joys were like our extended family. They convinced us that life on the road was "the thing" and we'd love it. I never believed anything anybody told me ever again. They recommended that we sign with One Nighters, an agency out of Nashville that they used. Our two groups chased each other all over the South and Midwest for a few months, playing the same clubs. We called it the Starvation Tour. We played in some of the worst places you ever saw, and the few months we did it seemed like years.

Our first gig on "the road" was at a place called the Colonial Gardens, in Louisville, Kentucky. We just knew that once we got out of Alabama, we would hit the big time immediately. Well, when we showed up to play this club, the manager informed us that no drinks were allowed on stage, as it wasn't "professional." The clincher was when he told us, "if you wanna get on my stage tomorrow night, you gotta have on uniforms." I guess our paisley Tom Jones shirts didn't quite make the fashion statement for us like they did for the Byrds, who we saw wearing similar ones on national TV. It suddenly dawned on me that maybe they had never heard of the Byrds at the Colonial Gardens or even the Rolling Stones, for that matter. We went out the next day anyhow and bought matching sport coats, "uniforms." That got us through our first club booking on "the road."

This was the first time we were able to play music full time. Boy, this is where you find out about "paying dues." After a few nights, we Men-its wrapped up our first enlightening road gig at the Colonial Gardens. By this time, our Nashville agency had another booking lined up for us on the other side of Kentucky. It was in Paducah, at a place called the Bunny Club. *Hot damn!* By that time, I had seen quite a few *Playboy* magazines and could just envision little scantily clad beauties in bunny suits with cotton tails pinned on, running around. Things were definitely picking up.

Well, when we got there, we discovered the club was in an old converted military Quonset hut. And the "bunny" part came from an over-stuffed rabbit-looking thing hanging from the ceiling. I remember the air was full of lint from the stuffing, which continued to fall out of that thing. We asked the club manager what time we were supposed to start playing; he said around midnight. We were expected to play till 5:00 in the morning! Good God-Da-Mighty! This was the first time I'd heard of an after-hours club, and I was not too keen on it.

Well, we played the first set to the bunny in the ceiling. Since nobody was there, we pretty much used the time as a rehearsal. Around 1:00 a.m., a few seasoned alcoholics and gamblers started to drift in. By 5:00, the clientele was in fine shape.

The club put us up in a motel that had a Chinese restaurant attached, and we got a discount on food. As we were counting pennies, we ate all our meals there. After a week of this fare, it's a wonder even today that I can stand to look at an egg roll.

For gig number three, our Nashville agency sent us to Bloomington, Illinois. Johnny Sandlin, Mabron McKinney, and I had our wives on the road with us by then and were riding six to the car in Johnny's Oldsmobile. Eddie Hinton drove his car by himself. None of us would ride with him because he would scream all the way. He said he was trying to keep his voice raspy for the gig. I'll tell you, there's nothing quite as disconcerting as riding in a car with a guy who's screaming.

We drove all night to Bloomington, Illinois, so we could save money on an extra day of motel rates. We pulled into town bright and early and went to a pay phone to call the club for directions. It was then that we discovered that there was no such club by that name in Bloomington, Illinois. It was several hours of hanging around the phone booth before we could reach anybody at the agency in Nashville. When we finally got somebody, they said "you're in Bloomington,

Illinois? You should be in Bloomington, *Indiana.* We must have made a mistake. Sorry about that."

I think it was along about that time that I started to have thoughts of mayhem. Luckily, there just wasn't anyone close by to kill. We got back in our cars and hauled ass more than two hundred miles to another state. We got there just in time to check into a motel and get our equipment set up for the gig. Bloomington, Indiana, turned out to be a college town, and, thank God, we found our audience. They loved every note we played. I've thought back a long time since then and have concluded that this might have been a turning point in my own career. We needed this morale booster, or I might have been on my way back to a South Alabama farm.

Around February of 1967 all our gigs fell out from under us, and we found ourselves at the Anchor Motel in Nashville, which was kind of our home base at the time. We'd be between gigs and just go to the Anchor, and then we'd play at a club in town called the Briar Patch. It was the only rock and roll bar in town at the time. It was a great place to play. Every night you'd look out in the audience to see what dignitaries might be out there, from Chet Atkins to John Loudermilk to dignitaries we didn't even know.

The road was rough. We didn't know that there would be down times like that, and here we were, three out of four of us in the band were married. We had wives to support. We didn't have any kids yet, but even when we were playing and getting paid weekly, we got real skinny and then all of a sudden there were no gigs for a couple of months and you know, we had some car payments and a few things in life that required cash. Eddie decided he didn't want any more of it. He wanted to get in the studio and be a session guitar player, so he left. He was our front man and main guitar player, but he went and moved to Muscle Shoals.

We ended up stranded in Johnny Sandlin's parents' garage where we auditioned singers, and guitar players. Every time we'd hear about somebody, we'd ask 'em to come and audition. That's how we found Pete Carr. He was sixteen years old and a guitar player, so we still needed a front man/singer. See, Eddie was both. So, it was taking two really good players to have equaled one Eddie Hinton. When Eddie left, that was the end of the 5 Men-Its.

Speaking of Eddie, books could be written about him alone! I've called Eddie the "Blackest white boy" I ever knew. He had a vocal and guitar style I haven't heard since. Eddie had Otis Redding down to a "T." He was always a little bit strange, which goes right along with geniuses, I think. Other than his music style, Eddie was in a club all by himself. No one else seemed to be invited. He was just very much a loner—harmless, but strange. Eddie got really strange in the last several years of his life. He was highly medicated during those years, but musically, he was all there.

Eddie's career had a lot of ups and downs. He went from being a first-call session player to literally sleeping on park benches. Maybe that was a form of success to him. I think being down and out was something Eddie thought you had to do to be authentic in playing R&B. Any way you look at it, Eddie never was really appreciated during his lifetime, and that's the way it usually is. He left us some years ago at the age of fifty-one, with some great unfinished demos in the can.

4

Like Sand through the
Hour Glass.

One bleak day in the middle of starvation, Duane Allman
called me up and said, "Man, it looks like the Allman Joys
are breaking up. We fired our bass player. Bill Connell, our
drummer, is getting drafted." He said, "Paul how would you
like to have me and Gregg in your band?" Well, it really
wasn't "my" band, but I thought it over thirty or forty sec-
onds and said, "Why, hell yes!" So, they drove to join us in
Decatur, Alabama, and we immediately started woodshedding in the Sandlins' garage.

The new band featured Gregg and Duane Allman,
Johnny Sandlin, myself, and Mabron "Wolf" McKinney. We
called him Wolf because he sported a full beard, which we
didn't see a lot of on guys our age. Of course, I played keyboards and guitar.

Duane and Gregg joining our band was a match made
in Heaven right there. We had a lot of the same songs that
they had. Just about all the Southern bands at that time
played "Stormy Monday," "Turn on Your Love Light" by

Bobby Bland, and a whole bunch of tunes like that which were just standards. Between the songs we knew and the songs they knew, we threw together enough for about two good sets. We did a lot of R&B covers and British covers. We did stuff like the Yardbirds' "Over Under Sideways Down," and "We Ain't got Nothing Yet" by Blues Magoos, plus a lot of songs that showed what the Allman Brothers would later sound like. We still didn't have a band name. We kicked the name Almanac around, but it never stuck.

"We were all good players," recalls Johnny Sandlin in *A Never-Ending Groove*, "but the band was even more special with Gregg's singing and Duane's guitar playing. The brothers were exciting, and Paul always played great and had his parts down. To me playing with these musicians was just a joy. Wolf McKinney was an extremely good bass player, and we would "lock" in together. I can't say enough good things about the band."

Not unlike the Five Minutes, we had nicknames for the members of the Hour Glass. I think I may be partly responsible for Duane's becoming "Skydog." We were in St. Louis, and this woman came out of a shop with a big ol' Afghan hound on a leash. You know they have that long, golden hair. I said, "Look at her! She's got Duane on a leash!" We immediately started calling him "The Dog," and he kept that nickname all through the Hour Glass years. Then, when he went to Muscle Shoals and became a session guitar player, he was recording with Wilson Pickett. Pickett started calling him "Skyman" because he was so far out. Somehow the two names turned into Skydog.

I gave Gregg the nickname "Grey Hog." He had a girl-friend in St. Louis who pronounced his name like that, "Grey-Hog." He just hated it. There were a few years that I didn't see him, and then I saw him somewhere and I said, "Hey there, Grey-Hog." He said, "Aw, shit, you remember that?" I said, "I'll never forget it, and I'll never let you forget it!" I think most of the ABB called him "The Coyote."

St. Louis had been a good town for the Allman Joys. The Allmans told us there was an area called Gaslight Square, which was sort of like Bourbon Street in New Orleans, and we could get a booking there. We'd been about three months without any work, and we were starving, so I said, "Let's get to St. Louis and quick!" Within two weeks we had our first booking at Pepe's-a-Go-Go in St. Louis. We played there for a month. I don't remember if we used the name Allman Joys or not. We had kicked a few names around. We all figured a new name was in order by now, but we hadn't settled into one.

During that month, Mabron McKinney, our bass player, was at the St. Louis airport when he ran into the Nitty Gritty Dirt Band. In those days (1967) you naturally noticed a fellow "long hair" and felt a natural kinship. Mabron had never heard of them because they hadn't had a big hit yet. They were on a promotion tour for their first LP. During the conversation, he invited them to come by Pepe's at Gaslight Square to hear us play while they were in town. This they did, accompanied by their manager, Bill McEuen. McEuen flipped out over the band. After the first set, he ran to the nearest pay phone and called someone at Liberty Records in Los Angeles and said, "Man, I've just discovered the next Rolling Stones!" Actually, he had discovered the future Allman Brothers Band.

He convinced us to come out to California and promised to get us a record deal. We did, he did, and the rest is history. He worked hard for us, so I have no bad words to say at all about Bill McEuen. After we arrived in L.A., we lived for a couple of weeks with the Nitty Gritty Dirt Band in their band house in the Hollywood Hills.

Nobody had a crystal ball in those days. You were just hitting on stuff. There was no mold. You just played whatever you felt like playing and hoped that something stuck when you threw it against the wall. Liberty Records tried hard to change our image, style- and music-wise. In fact, on the first album we did, they picked out some demos and cut some stuff. They had horns and Black chick singers behind us and wanted a kind of Motown-sounding band. And they wanted Gregg to hold a mike, get out from behind the organ, come out and hold a mike and have a back-up band, like a "soul review" or something. And I mean, they just couldn't see what we were doing, what we *were*. We were pretty much what you'd expect the early Allman Brothers Band to sound like. We had five pieces and were doing a lot of the tunes the Brothers later became famous for. Duane had picked up slide by this time, and "Statesboro Blues" was the first song he ever played slide on. We were doing that just like the Brothers later did it. We were doing "Stormy Monday Blues," which became a Brothers standard. A lot of people to this day think that they wrote it, but we had played that song through two or three different bands. We were a Southern rock band, but that didn't work well with what Liberty wanted us to be. Duane was hard to please, and he wasn't getting the respect he thought he deserved. You couldn't control Duane; he was the most headstrong person I ever saw. Most of us just had that "good ol' boy" attitude, but you couldn't tell Duane what to do. We were just in our early twenties and living in Hollywood. Who from Alabama or Florida or the South wouldn't want to be living in Hollywood? It was a dream, so whatever they suggested, whatever they wanted to do in the studio, we did. We jumped for it. None of us really had studio experience.

They wanted a soul singer with a back-up band. About the first gig we played out there was sort of a showcase where we played in front of the guy who was going to produce our stuff. They had talked Gregg into holding a mike and walking out on a runway. I remember the song was "A Change Is Gonna Come" by Sam Cooke, and, of course, Gregg could sing that song into the ground. I mean, we could just kill that song. So, Gregg's holding the mike and steps away from the keyboard—I guess they were expecting him to be Tom Jones—and he walks out on that runway. He got about a good ten feet out in front of the band and looked around. He could see us out of the corner of his eye; we were way back there and he was way out on this runway. I felt sorry for him because his knees were shaking, and I swear to God, I'd never seen anybody so scared. One of the first notes out of his mouth, his voice cracked.

That showcase did not make a good impression. In fact, the producer didn't even want to sign us. The manager convinced him to come and see us again. Gregg put his foot down, though. "No more of this damn runway shit!" he said. "Just leave us alone, let us play." And so, we played, and, of course, they signed us. No more of the Tom Jones stuff.

Chuck Leavell says that he was a regular audience member for the Hour Glass gigs at the Brandon Armory in Tuscaloosa. "I was blown away by the band. I recall that was the first time I ever saw a guitarist use a fuzz effect pedal. Duane had one, it was called a Fuzz Face, a round floor pedal that distorted the signal in a psychedelic kind of way."

We cut one LP for Liberty, then Mabron McKinney left the group. When Wolf left, Gregg and Duane wanted us to hire the Allman Joys' bass player, Bob Keller. That was okay with us because we knew him from playing together in the old days. He was a great musician and showman, so he joined the band. We got along great. My wife and I became good friends with Bob and his wife.

Publicly, Bob and his wife always acted just hunky dory and didn't seem to have any problems. But one time, we had two or three nights booked at the Whisky a Go Go, and our equipment was set up. It got to be about an hour before show time, and everyone was accounted for—except Bob Keller. We had no idea where he was and thought maybe he'd fallen off a mountain. We looked everywhere for him, but we had to play in an hour. As luck would have it, sixteen-year-old Pete Carr was out there visiting us at the time. So, we grabbed Pete and asked him to play bass. Pete was a great guitar player, but he told us he had never played bass before. I said, "You will tonight!" He played that night and did a good job.

A few weeks later, Bob Keller popped back up in L.A. and said, "Hi guys!" He thought we'd just welcome him back, but we did not. Pete was our new bass player. We found out that Bob and his wife had been having problems, and Keller had hopped on a plane and flown back to Daytona to see her.

After that, Pete was our bass player for the rest of the time that the Hour Glass was together even though he had never played bass before. However, after a little bit of arm-twisting, he jumped right in and continued on bass until the end of the group in 1968. We cut one more LP for Liberty in 1968.

At this time, "surf music" was the thing on the west coast—the Beach Boys, Jan and Dean—and here we were, a band of Southern cats with a blues-oriented sound, like you might expect the predecessor to the Allman Brothers band to be. You might say we were the first "Southern rock" band in the classic sense of the word, but the term had not been coined yet. The producer and record company didn't have a clue as to what to do with us. Our producer had just had a few hits with Jan and Dean, Bobby Vee, and the like. Because we had a "Black" or "blues" sound, he kept referring to us as a "Motown" band. Wrong section of the country. Our first record was filled with horns and Black chick singers. We were just eager to please. Anything they suggested, we went along with. We were just a bunch of country boys, what did we know? We did know how to make music. Most of the stuff they had us play on those records, we never played live. We had a set of mostly blues and R&B-sounding stuff that we had put together during the past year together and inherited from past bands we had all been a part of.

With the Hour Glass, I was playing the Hammond organ, so when we were recording the first album, the producer brought in a session piano player. They said his name was Mac, that he was from New Orleans, kind of a weird guy, but that we would like him. He was good. He didn't come in and try to show off. He was pushing me to play more piano. I didn't give it a whole lot of thought. I was already playing organ, and he only played on one song, "Nothing but Tears." That was 1967. Fast forward to the early 1970s, around 1972. Dr. John had moved to Macon, and I had started playing with him. We were onstage one night when it hit me like a bolt out of the blue—*that's the guy who played on our album!* It's funny what a small world it really is.

The Hour Glass played all up and down the California coast, hitting all the biggest clubs—Fillmore West, the Avalon Ballroom, the Whisky a Go Go—as well as serving as opening act at stadium concerts. We were on the bill with bands like Jefferson Airplane, Buffalo Springfield, the Animals, and Janis Joplin with Big Brother and the Holding Company. The Fillmore was beginning to be noticed in all the rock magazines as the headquarters for the 'Frisco bands like Jefferson Airplane, the Grateful Dead, and Big Brother. Bill Graham owned the club and managed the Airplane and several other bands who played there. Bill didn't yet have the legendary status he acquired after his death; he was just a guy who gave the bands a place to play and gave the people what they wanted to hear. He seemed to know what those fans wanted though.

At the time, I never gave much thought to Bill, no more than any other club owner. I do know that he was a fan of the Hour Glass. He kept having us back at the Fillmore even though we didn't have a charted record. One thing I remember about Bill was, one night after a weekend at the Fillmore, we were struggling with my Hammond, carrying it down those steep steps in front of the club. A bunch of stragglers were hanging around after closing time. He yelled out "Give those cowboys some room. They just played their asses off, and now they're trying to get their own gear out." I don't know why, but he seemed impressed by that. I've toted it many times since.

We were practically the house band at Whisky a Go Go. It was a prestigious place to play back then. We sort of started a custom of jam sessions when we worked there. The biggest acts in the country, when in town, would come out to hear us play and sit in. One such unforgettable night, Janis Joplin, Eric Burdon, Steve Stills, Neil Young, Buddy Miles, and Paul Butterfield joined us on stage there. The club had to pull the power plug to stop us that night because there was a 2:00 a.m. closing curfew. We had opened for most of those acts, so we had developed a reputation of sorts—all without the benefit of a hit record, which we knew was necessary to help us break outside of California.

When we were in Hollywood, the TV show *Lost in Space* was popular. We got hired to play at a private Halloween party for June Lockhart at her house. She had a teenaged daughter named Annie, who was about fourteen or fifteen at the time, the same age as Angela Cartwright, who played June's daughter Penny on the show. The two girls were running buddies together. We played the party at June's house, and they were the most gracious hosts you could imagine. They just loved our band. At the end of the party, June said that she hoped we would come out to the set some time. Of course, we just ate that up. One early morning, just a few days later, I got a call. I was used to Gregg calling me in the middle of the night and at all hours to come and get him out of jail, so, when the phone rang at 6 a.m., I was livid. You just don't ring a musician's phone that early in the morning without suffering the consequences. I grabbed the phone and yelled into it, "This better be God damned good!" And this woman's soft voice says, "Paul? This is June Lockhart." I fumbled around, embarrassed. "I was just wondering," she said, "if you and the guys would like to come out to the set today." I said, "Absolutely!" I got ahold of everybody, herded them up, and we went out there. We watched them film, then took a little break and went outside to have some pictures made. There were all sorts of props sitting around outside. We saw the robot and everything. The only person we didn't meet was Jonathan Harris, who played Dr. Smith. "Don't worry," June whispered to me, "his character is the same on or off camera."

As an interesting aside, the episode they were filming that day was called "Junk Yard in Space," and it was their very last episode. I don't know if they knew that at the time or not. After that, we invited Billy Mumy (Will Robinson) and Angela Cartwright to come to the Whisky a Go Go to hear us play. We kept running into Angela at different events.

We had run into her about the second week we were in Los Angeles. We were booked to play a press party that Danny Thomas was throwing. It was to announce a new show that he was doing, and it was at the Beverly Hilton Hotel. We were thrown right into the middle of it, and it doesn't get more Hollywood than that. Every television star in LA was at that event. I couldn't believe it: Martin Landau and Barbara Bain from *Mission Impossible* were there. Frank Sutton who played Sgt. Carter on *Gomer Pyle USMC* was there. He liked the band a lot. When we were playing, he sat right under us to watch. They had given us one of those extremely nice rooms as a green room, and before we went on, or maybe it was on a break, a knock came at the door. It was a pretty woman who exclaimed, "Hi, I'm Tippi Hedren, and I've got to pee." She dashed into the bathroom and didn't close the door or anything. Welcome to Hollywood! Of course, she was riding high at the time as star of Hitchcock's *The Birds*.

Chad Everett was there too. It was a who's who of 1967 television. We did a lot of shows where Hollywood folks would attend. We did an Artists & Models Ball, and Adam West was there in his Batman costume.

We got invited to a movie premiere of a film John Lennon had appeared in called *How I Won the War*. The premier was done up Hollywood style with the limos, the red carpet, the whole nine yards. Well, we couldn't very well drive up in a 1962 Pontiac, so Johnny Sandlin, Pete Carr, and I chipped in to rent a limo one way. It's not important how you drive away from a place, it's how you arrive. First impressions, you know. When we drove up, all these little teeny boppers swamped the limo. They didn't know who we were; they just thought we must be rock and roll royalty. Everybody was yelling "Who are they?" If we'd told them, they probably would have left. Duane and Gregg had rented their own limo and charged it to the band. We were all led through the crowd and went in. Paul Revere & the Raiders were seated right in front of us. There were all sorts of rock stars there that night. We watched the movie and stayed inside the theater afterward until most of the crowd had dispersed. When it was all clear, we came out of the theater and thumbed a ride back home.

There is one story that has been told many times in the past—incorrectly. Here's the true version: Back in the sixties, the Troubadour in LA was known as a folk music club more than anything. They let us rehearse there during the afternoons when they were closed. I had an electric guitar strapped on, and I went to adjust the mike stand. My hands stuck to the stand, and I couldn't turn it loose. I was getting a good healthy dose of electricity, jerking around onstage, and the band started laughing. They thought I was cutting up. I was yelling, "I'm dying here!" It knocked me unconscious, and, when I fell off the stage, my guitar came unplugged, saving my life. When I came to, my long hair was stuck all over the guitar strings. I had never been electrocuted like that before, but that's how it really happened. Others have told the story before to rewrite history, but I'm the one who got jolted, so I know what really happened.

I have been asked just who forced the Hour Glass guys to wear the costumes we wore, the psychedelic clothes and Sandlin's confederate uniform. I just say they need to remember that this was at the time the Beatles had out *Sgt. Pepper*, the biggest musical statement ever. So, we were in our Sgt. Pepper period.

Our set list began to look more and more like what the future Allman Brothers Band set list would look like. Duane and I played double guitars. "Tobacco Road" was our show closer, and we just rocked the stage. Duane threw his guitar into the air, and it'd come down feeding back. I was kicking the organ; it was just chaos. We left everything in a heap, and the crowd loved it. This was before Pete Townsend was wrecking his gear and before Jimi Hendrix set his guitar on fire.

During those days in Los Angeles, Duane was the visual focus of the band. He had the commanding personality. When there's somebody like that in a group you realize, "We gotta do what he says because he's the stuff," you know? He's the first person I ever saw who looked that way, talked that way, played that way. He was really an American original. Unfortunately, Liberty Records didn't see him that way.

They kept pushing Gregg, making him front and center in press photos, or making him seem larger in photos. Gregg was their focus and the rest of us were an afterthought.

The Hour Glass released a second album with Liberty Records, *Power of Love*, and the single on the same day. It was a good record with a full color record sleeve and everything, but it wasn't embraced by the public. We went on tour around February of 1968. I don't think *The Power of Love* had been out more than a couple of weeks. "Tour" is a bit generous because we were mostly playing little ol' honky-tonks. But we played the Comic Book Club in Jacksonville, where the Allman guys were already pretty well known. We were in our twenties, and there was a younger band there called the One Percent. They were our opening act. We were in our dressing rooms and heard the band strike up. I heard something that sounded familiar. I stuck my head out the door to hear better, and they were playing a song from our *Power of Love* album, the record that we were there to promote. The next song was another one from our record. They played our whole album during their set—and sounded better than we did! When we got up to play, we were playing the same songs, but the people who were there didn't know anything about these albums. Ronnie Van Zant, Gary Rossington, and Allen Collins were in the One Percent. (Flash forward to 1975, and I was out in San Diego with Marshall Tucker. Lynyrd Skynyrd was there, and I reminded Ronnie of that story. He kind of hung his head and was embarrassed. "Man," he said, "I'd hoped you'd forget that. We were just

Paul Hornsby

kids. We idolized y'all, and that's why we did it." "It's okay,"
I said. "you did 'em better than we did.")

After our second album came out, we even went to
Muscle Shoals with our own money and cut a few things to
take back out to them to show the way we wanted to be recorded. It always puzzled me how so much music could come
out of an area that had no nightclubs or places for musicians
to play. You couldn't even buy a drink of liquor in the Shoals
for a long time; you had to drive across the Tennessee state
line for that. Somehow though, those ol' boys up there laid
down some basic, honest music. I never heard anything fancy
there, but it doesn't have to be. They know how to back up
a singer/musician and allow them to shine through and get
the most out of them. So, we were happy to record there.

Upon hearing the tapes, the producer thought they were
horrible! Well, those same tapes later appeared on a couple
of the *Duane Allman Anthology* albums. There was the "B.B.
King Medley," "Been Gone Too Long," and I think maybe
another. These tapes weren't a big stretch from the stuff the
Allman Brothers would later do. What I'm getting at is that
finally in the 70s we could explore our Southern roots and
record music that we had grown up hearing. We were later
given a chance to do that in Macon, Georgia. It seemed just
a short time after the first Allman and Tucker albums that
the music term "Southern rock" was first used. Lynyrd
Skynyrd even had the Macon connection, with their manager, Alan Walden. Macon had previously been the proving
ground for Little Richard, Otis Redding, and James Brown,
making it pretty much the home of Southern rock.

With things at a standstill at Liberty, we had become disillusioned with the whole Los Angeles thing. Duane wanted to come back east. We did try it back in the old haunts again for a month or two, but it just didn't work out. The Hour Glass disbanded by late summer of 1968.

Right after we came back from California (and before we broke up), we played at the Briar Patch. (We started using the name "Allman Joys" again because that's what people back East knew us as.) That afternoon we set up our equipment for the show. There was a waitress there who was a pretty rough customer. Duane had a bunch of these cracker balls that pop like a firecracker when you throw them or step on them. He had gone into the women's restroom and put these things on the underside of the commode lid so when someone sat on it, they would go off. Back in high school we used to toss a few on the floor when the hall was crowded during class changes, and the principal would jump out of his chair and just have a fit. But that afternoon at the Briar Patch we were setting up our equipment and we heard this explosion—*Pop! Pop! Pop!* That tough waitress came out of the bathroom cussing and with her pants pulled halfway up. She had a switchblade and was swinging it back and forth. She said, "If I catch the son of a bitch that did this, I'm gonna cut his heart out and eat it!" It got real quiet, and Duane got real scarce.

Lots of people have asked me about working with Duane Allman. Duane was one of the few musicians I would go as far as to say was a genius. He was an inventor with the guitar, which is quite different from being an imitator. He wasn't just a great musician—he was smart intellectually and charismatic. That's just something you have and can't be explained. You've either got it or you don't.

There were two things Duane Allman was always dodging the law over: BB guns and firecrackers. Bill Connell played drums for the Allman Joys, and he tells about one of their first gigs when they drove through the Shenandoah Forest. Duane was shooting off a bunch of firecrackers when the weeds caught on fire. The flames headed toward the forest; they were about to burn down the Shenandoah forest. They hurried up the road to the station and reported seeing a fire. What they didn't say was that they started it. Bill can really tell that story in detail. That was the first time Duane almost got in trouble over firecrackers. Luckily, the rangers were able to come and put out the fire.

Later, we were in St. Louis, and Duane had a BB gun, shooting out the streetlights. Like Bourbon Street, this street was lit up at night with real gas lights. Duane and Gregg had an apartment they were staying in above Pepe's a Go Go. Three of us were married, so we were staying in the Windsor Hotel. Duane was shooting out the lights, and a big knock came on the door. It was the police looking for Duane and his BB gun, but Duane had opened the window and stashed the BB gun out on the roof of the house. He said, "I don't have a BB gun. You can search if you want to."

Before we went to St. Louis, Johnny Sandlin's parents were so good at putting up with us rehearsing in their garage. Mr. Sandlin had some pure-bred hunting dogs, and he was always telling Duane, "Don't be shooting that gun around my little old dogs." "Oh no," Duane would say, "I'd never do that!" But as soon as Mr. Sandlin wasn't looking, he'd be shooting again.

Duane had something going all the time; he had so much creative energy. If he wasn't shooting firecrackers, if you went to visit him, he'd have a guitar across his lap while he was reading a book. He'd read a while, stop and pick a while, and then read some more. His mind never stopped.

5

Under the Sign of Capricorn

In summer 1968, after the Hour Glass broke up, I went back to Tuscaloosa to sort of regroup. Duane moved to Muscle Shoals like Eddie Hinton had done and was playing guitar on some stuff. Pete Carr and Johnny Sandlin went down to Miami to work on sessions as well. I moved back to Tuscaloosa, and it was a great musician's town, a town where you could find a musician if you needed one. A prime example of that from years later, was when Charlie Daniels called me after the first album we cut, *Fire on the Mountain.*

"Paul, man," he said, "I'm gonna have to find me a bass player. My bass player's quitting. Do you know any good bass players? We're on the way to Tuscaloosa to do a show, and the bass player's given two-week's notice."

"Well," I said, "since you're going to Tuscaloosa, the best bass player I know that you need to talk to is Charlie Hayward." The way I remember this now, as soon as they pulled into town—this was well before cell phone days—Charlie went to a pay phone, called up Charlie Hayward, and hired him on the spot. Of course, Hayward was ready to go. He packed his bag and his bass and got on the bus that night. That was about 1975, and he's been with the CDB ever since. That's how he was hired. That's called being in the right place at the right time.

Tuscaloosa was always filled with wonderful musicians. Bill Stewart, the drummer who played on a lot of Capricorn stuff, was living there, and you might as well say he was from there; Eddie Hinton; and, of course, Tippy Armstrong, who became a renowned session player in Muscle Shoals; Johnny Townsend from the Sanford/Townsend Band; and, of course, a sixteen-year-old piano player named Chuck Leavell, to name just a handful.

I moved back there, and there was this club in town, just across the bridge from Tuscaloosa, called the Chef Lounge that featured a sort of a loosely held together house band. Every one of these musicians, at one time or another, drifted in there and was playing. In fact, on any given Friday or Saturday night, they'd be there playing and jamming and stuff, just a who's who of musicians. I moved back there and moved my Hammond organ right on in there. This was an obvious next stop-off for me. Some of the most magical musical moments of my life were spent at that place. Those musicians will always be like a family to me. Eventually, I tried to consolidate the group into a more stable organization than the jam band, and the result was a group consisting of myself on organ and guitar, Bill Stewart on drums, Glen Butts on guitar, Richard Kent on vocals, Charlie Hayward on bass, and Chuck Leavell, who was about to be a high school senior, on piano and vocals. I believe we kept this lineup longer than any other previous incarnations of the group, which was called South Camp.

To this day every time I see Chuck Leavell, one of us will mention "Nadine, My Darling." Back when we were in South Camp together, we were playing at the Chef and this drunk came up to me. I mean, he was drunk out of his mind. He came up and said, "Play 'Nadine, My Darling.'" "I'm sorry, man," I said, "we don't know that." A couple of songs later, he came back and asked for it again. Every time he came back, he was drunker than before. Finally, he came up and laid a twenty-dollar bill on my organ and asked for us to play that song. In 1968, twenty dollars spoke real loud. I looked at him and said, "For twenty dollars, I'll write you a song!" I asked him to hum it, so he did and started singing, "Nadine my darling, children at your feet…." From then on, every time we played "Lady Madonna" we sang "Nadine, My Darling."

We had that band playing together for about nine months. I was teaching guitar lessons and making a living again. I wasn't living in Hollywood in the bright lights, but I was eating better than I had in Hollywood anyway. After about eight months of that, Duane called me from Muscle Shoals one day and said, "Hey man, I want to cut some de-mos. Would you come up here and play some keyboards on some of them for me?" And he added, "I've been playing some sessions, and some people at Atlantic listened to my playing and they want to see if I can cut an album as an artist, maybe." So, I drove up there and was up there two or three days. Johnny Sandlin was there, and Berry Oakley showed up (Duane had just met him down in Florida). Berry wound up playing bass, Johnny Sandlin on drums, and I played keys. Duane, of course, played guitar and sang. We cut several demos and stuff that Rick Hall produced, and most of these tunes later wound up on some of the Duane Allman anthology records, the very songs we demo-ed while we were there. We cut "Happily Married Man," "Goin' Down Slow," "Bad News," and "No Money Down."

Things happened fast during those days. Phil Walden came in; he wanted to sign Duane and put a band together around him, and he asked me and Johnny to play. Essentially, he wanted to put the Hour Glass back together. Now, Gregg wasn't there. I didn't ask where he was, but this was Duane's band, and it was going to be the Duane show. Before, it had always been the Gregg show. We'd just spent two years in the Hour Glass, and those were the stepping stones, as you might say. I'd already stepped on that stone, and I wasn't ready to be back in the Hour Glass. I was just trying to move on because there comes a time when you just need to quit whippin' that dead horse. But Phil insisted, saying, "No man, you've gotta play with Duane." "No, no, no," I said, "I don't have to, no."

Finally, Phil says to me and Sandlin, "Well, if y'all won't play in this band with Duane, I'm building a studio in Macon and I want to have a house band, a staff band. Would y'all consider being in the house band?" I asked him where the studio would be. He said, "It's in Macon." And I remember asking him, "Macon? Where's that? What state is that in?" He explained where it was in Georgia and said, "You know, Little Richard is from there, Otis Redding is from there." There was no reason we should have ever heard of Macon at that time. Nothing had ever happened there; there had never really been a music scene there. Little Richard and Otis were from Macon, but they had to go somewhere else to make it in the business. He didn't even have a record company—it was just a studio, and he was almost finished building it. Every week Phil would call, and the deal got a little better and a little better. He could talk you into anything, but I had started having some amount of success. Here was a band I had with Chuck Leavell; we were playing regularly, and I was teaching guitar lessons and eating regularly. Having to quit and move again didn't appeal to me. It took about two months before I found myself in Macon, Georgia, working down at Capricorn along with Johnny Sandlin on drums, Pete Carr on guitar, and Robert Popwell on bass. We became the original rhythm section at Capricorn Studio. We were trying to pattern ourselves after the success of the legendary Muscle Shoals rhythm section and my heroes, Booker T. and the M.G.s, the staff band at Stax. Of course, Johnny, Pete, and I had played together for years in the Hour Glass. Popwell was recommended to Phil by Duane. He was from Daytona. Man, could he ever play bass. We called him "Bumble Bass." His brother was a well-known actor named Johnny Popwell. He was in a movie called *The Night is a Lonely Hunter* (1968), starring Alan Arkin and Sondra Locke, who went on to marry Clint Eastwood. He was also in *Deliverance* (1972) with Burt Reynolds. Robert might not have been the first, but he was the first *I ever saw* who played "slap" bass. I thought it was cool as hell. Not every bass player can do that.

Phil Walden had charisma. He understood us. I wish we'd had him two years earlier because he got it. The folks in California did not get it, but Phil could see it. Bill McEuen got it. He tried. He saw the importance of Duane. But the producer at Liberty didn't have a clue and looked completely past Duane.

It's probably because of each other that Johnny Sandlin and I wound up at Capricorn. We had been compadres during the Men-Its days and then the Hour Glass. He convinced me to make the move when Phil Walden offered us the job at Capricorn Studios. We became the two staff producers for Capricorn Records after starting out as session players in the house band at the studio. Some projects just fell to him and some to me. I think the only project we ever coproduced was the Kitty Wells LP, *Forever Young*. We started that one together, but I then finished it alone. I think it was too "country" for Johnny's taste. I believe I had more of a country background than he. As for the rock things we did, I believe all our backgrounds came in handy, for there were equal parts of country, blues, jazz, what have you, that made up the Southern rock genre.

At first, I was the resident studio piano player, backing various acts that Walden had under contract. Within a year, I was asked to produce a local Macon group named the Boogie Chillun. During the recording of that album, the band broke up and reformed two or three times. I finally called up Chuck Leavell and some other Tuscaloosa friends and asked them to come over and finish up the album. The final version of the album saw the band name changed to Sundown. That was the first album I produced.

When we came to Macon in 1969, Capricorn didn't have the label established yet. I believe it was several months before they had a label, but Atlantic talked them into having one. The first records that they put out were on Atco/Atlantic, and they had "Capricorn Series" printed on them. So, us guys, the Capricorn Rhythm Section, put out a single, and I believe it was the first record on the Capricorn label. There was a dance craze at the time called "the Chicken," and Booker T. & the MGs put out an instrumental called "Southern Fried." Well, we figured we were a lot like Booker T., so we got in the studio and came up with a record called "Pully Bone." We didn't have a name for the group, but we had to call it something on the record, so we just called it "Macon." I don't know whose idea it was, but it sounded as good as anything else. It got some radio play here and there, and it hit biggest in Miami of all places. The b-side was called "Ripple Rap." We drank a lot of Ripple wine back then because it was cheap, about a dollar a gallon. That's about all we could afford. The "rap" in the title is not to be confused with what they call rap today, the talking with music behind it. I don't like it. I don't get it. It's not music, it's just noise, and it's not even good noise. And they play it so loud.

We were all hanging out, and by this time, Duane had talked Gregg into to moving back from Los Angeles. They'd gotten the Allman Brothers Band together. Duane fleshed the group out and got what he wanted. All of that happened fast, and the brothers relocated from Florida to Macon. It went from them asking Sandlin and me to play to two months later, he's got Butch and Jaimoe and all these guys. Jaimoe was already in town because he'd played with Otis, with Percy Sledge, with all these R&B acts. Jaimoe fit right in with Butch, so the original Allman Brothers Band formed in Macon in about two months. We had our studio guys, and we had the Allman Brothers Band, and we were all like one big family, really. When we weren't jamming in the studio, we were at each other's apartments, just hanging out. That's all there was to do since nobody had any money. Sunday afternoons, we usually wound up on a school playground somewhere, playing cork ball. That was a sport I'd never heard of. It was something Duane came up with or something he'd played—you had broomsticks for a bat and a cork with a penny taped on the small end to balance it out. You would hit that cork, and how many bases you took depended on how far you hit it. You know, you didn't have to really run and get thrown out. You just had to hit the cork a certain distance, and then you got to take so many bases.

For a while, our Capricorn Rhythm Section played on records for R&B artists like Eddie Floyd and Arthur Conley and folk acts like Livingston Taylor. I settled into daily studio work and became studio manager at Capricorn. In addition to playing sessions, there were artists coming through who occasionally asked me to join them for tours. I'd cut sessions during the week and fly out to do gigs with them on weekends. Livingston Taylor and Dr. John were among my favorites. I like to say that I got a master's degree playing B-3 behind Dr. John. Playing with him was like a reward, like a musical scholarship. Mac was the only guy I ever saw who could play and talk at the same time. I remember playing some place, and there was a piano in the dressing room. He was in there, just tearing it up. Somebody was talking to him, and he had his head turned and was deep into the conversation while he was playing his ass off. What a character. He'd come out onstage wearing all these furs and feathers, and he had a sack full of glitter, "gris gris" that he tossed onto people. We played a lot of shows with the Allman Brothers, and Red Dog (roadie Joseph Campbell) was always bitching about all the glitter that got down in between Gregg's organ keys.

Once I flew with Dr. John from Miami to Puerto Rico for the Mar y Sol Pop Festival in San Juan. It was pretty much a fiasco as far as organization was concerned. They treated us musicians like kings, but the promoters had ripped off a bunch of people. After the festival, their tickets to return home were no good. When we flew out, there were people there sleeping on the floor of the airport because they didn't have tickets to get home.

The first Capricorn Rhythm Section lasted a year or two until Capricorn started signing a lot of bands. The more bands they signed, the less work there was for a rhythm section. So, the first of us they let go was Pete Carr. He went straight to Muscle Shoals. I can remember calling either Roger Hawkins or Jimmy Johnson from Pete's kitchen one day. I said, "I'd love for you to give Pete Carr a listen. He's been with us over a year, and we're about to fold up the rhythm section. I think he'd fit right in there." That was kind of a call of introduction, and Pete went right to work there, playing on a lot of giant records. I didn't know what happened to Popwell at first. We kind of lost track of him, but we found out he had gone right to work with the Jazz Crusaders, later known as the Crusaders.

6

Macon Magic

Even though it was referred to as Capricorn "Studios," there was one recording room. I think the "studios" reference came from the fact that there was a side room left as a rehearsal area. We always thought of turning that into Studio B but never did. I don't have actual dimensions, but I would have to say the studio room was probably twenty-five by forty feet. It was a good-sized room, and most of the space was never utilized. Probably the best use of all that space might have been having one group's equipment set up at one end while another was set up at the other end. The control room was sizable; Tom Hidley designed it in the early 70s, and, at that time, it was the biggest control room he had done.

Bands recorded around the clock. Somebody would be recording during the day, and another crew would come in at night. Johnny Sandlin and I produced most of those sessions. In our younger days, we would fight over who would get the night sessions. Then, as we got older and settled in, we'd fight over who would get the daytime sessions. I never could understand how in Nashville they could go in at nine or ten in the morning and record music. I could never do that.

When I was a young engineer at Capricorn, before I'd done any Tucker records or anything, I got a call one night from Phil. Well, at the time I was sick in bed with the flu. Phil told me there was a singer playing down at Mercer in the cafeteria. Somebody in Nashville called and requested that we send somebody out there to hear him. The Allman Brothers had not hit yet, but news had been circulating that there was a record company being formed in Macon. At the time, everybody wanted to be James Taylor, and "Fire and Rain" was the biggest thing going. So, everybody who came to Capricorn to audition would be carrying an acoustic guitar. We could pretty much count on hearing "Fire and Rain" right after they took that Martin or whatever out of the case. "Oh," we'd say, "it's just another folk singer."

I didn't want to tell Phil I was too sick to go, so I said I'd go. I got there a little late. I went in, and this guy was sitting there playing an acoustic guitar. I heard him play a couple of songs, and they were okay. One of them was about stealing peanut butter in a grocery store or some such. I talked to him during his break, and we talked about people we knew in common. He told me he was from Alabama, and I asked what city. He said Mobile, and I said, "Then you probably know the Wet Willie guys." He said that he did, so we talked about them for a few minutes. We exchanged a few pleasantries, and it came time for him to go back up to play. I told him I was sorry, but I wasn't feeling well and wouldn't be able to stay, so I said goodbye. He went back up to play, and I went to the bathroom to throw up, then went back home and got in the bed. Phil called me the next day and asked if I went to see the guy and what I thought of him. I said, "Oh, he's just another fucking folk singer." Phil said, "What was his name?" "I believe his name was Buffett...yeah, Jimmy Buffett," I said.

A few years ago, we were at the Alabama Music Hall of Fame banquet and we sat with Norbert Putnam. He was a part of the original FAME session crew, the same group that Jerry Carrigan and David Briggs were in. He went up to Nashville and ended up playing on the road with Elvis for years. At the table, I had just met Norbert; I don't think he knew my credentials, and I was just getting to know his. We were talking, and I said, "Norbert, I want you to know I did you a big favor." He looked at me like, "What the...?" I told him the Buffett story, and he fell out on the floor laughing. You see, Norbert Putnam was the Jimmy Buffett's producer on "Margaritaville." He produced all of Jimmy's hits. But like I told Norbert, "I did not hear 'Margaritaville' that night."

Capricorn Recording Studio and the business office of Walden & Associates on Cotton Avenue were two totally different entities. We didn't jive at all. Capricorn was the record company and there was the booking agency, Paragon, was also there, as well as Phil Walden & Associates management. They didn't come down and bother us and we didn't bother them. We might as well have been in two separate cities. One thing I'll say about Phil Walden to his credit, among many other things, is that he didn't look over our shoulders down there. He never came over to tell us what to do and what not to do. He gave us the freedom to spend as much time as we needed recording. I don't think anybody ever kept up with the hours. He would charge some of the recording costs to the bands, but nobody kept up with it too much. That was something we didn't have to worry about. He just said, "Go in there and cut me some great music." And that's what we tried to do. He only came in the studio a handful of times, usually if there was a dignitary in town like Jimmy Carter, who wanted to see the studio. If he'd been in there during recording, we would have frozen up. It'd be like trying to take a leak with ten people behind you in line.

Phil had his gifts, but I don't think he could tell a quarter note from a whole note. He probably couldn't play a single chord on a guitar. But he knew what he liked. There were a lot of great artists and songs he let slip by that I think he shouldn't have, but the great thing about him was, whatever he believed in, he could sell it. And he had charisma, kind of like what Duane Allman had. He could just make you like something. He'd make you like it, and then he'd sell it to you. He was a great businessman.

Frank Fenter was the vocal side of the two. He had a lot of energy. He was Phil's henchman; if there was something Phil didn't want to do, he'd put Frank on it. It sometimes made Frank unpopular, but he was doing everything Phil asked of him. It took me a while to get to know Frank Fenter. I didn't like him when he first came here. I don't know if he felt like he had something to prove, but we had a studio band, and he worked us like a rented mule. We were drawing a weekly check, and he liked to have worked us to death. He'd have us working until one or two in the morning and we had to be back in there at nine. After the first month, we

finally just told him that we had to have time off. We're going to work certain hours, we're going to take the evenings
off and get a good night's sleep, and we're not coming in for
another twelve hours. We were recording songwriter demos
on every songwriter who ever came to Macon. He had us
churning these demos out and hoping that something would
stick to the wall. He was all business, and it took him a while
to come off that, but when he did, we became friendlier and
more like buddies.

We became good friends after Capricorn shut down.
Frank would come to my studio, Muscadine, and there was
a band or two out of Atlanta that he wanted to cut stuff on.
He'd bring them to my studio, and it was more like a meeting of peers. I truly enjoyed Frank's company in the end days
there. Then Phil got a new offer from Polygram and made
one phone call to Frank. I think Frank left the phone off the
hook and the motor running and took off to work with Phil.
Frank didn't last too much longer after that. He died on July
23, 1985. Capricorn had several other employees who were
pivotal to its success, including Dick Wooley, a hard worker
in charge of promotions, and Mike Highland, who did publicity.

In 1970, Johnny Sandlin produced Johnny Jenkins's
Ton-Ton Macoute!, which was originally supposed to be a
Duane Allman solo LP. We cut a bunch of stuff with Duane
singing. It was less than great, but I didn't think it was bad.
The truth is, it wasn't so much that they were going to make
a Duane solo album as it was that Jerry Wexler just wanted
to see what Duane could do. They had yet to meet Gregg

and wanted to see what Duane's limitations were—they wanted to see if he could sing. There weren't many recordings of Duane singing. He never really liked to sing and knew he'd never be the singer Gregg was, just like he knew Gregg would never be the guitar player that Duane was. Duane saw the writing on the wall, and he was never one to let dust settle on him. He had already started getting some guys together for a band. In fact, he already had Jaimoe and Berry Oakley. Berry ended up playing on the demos, but Jaimoe was not on them. Johnny Sandlin played drums. So, Duane, Berry, Sandlin and I played on Duane's demos. We were recording on 8-tracks, which was pretty much state of the art at the time. These recordings were made at FAME Studio in Muscle Shoals.

With the momentum picking up for the Allman Brothers Band and no longer a need for a Duane solo album, Johnny Jenkins, the guitarist and singer who had helped launch Otis Redding's career, took over *Ton-Ton Macoute!* We added his vocals to many of the tracks, creating a classic album that many are unaware of. The version of Dr. John's "I Walk on Gilded Splinters" is perfection, and many artists have sampled the drum track for their records. We recorded a new version of Taj Mahal's "Leavin Trunk" and Jackie Avery's "Blind Bats and Swamp Rats." There was a John D. Loudermilk track or two that we had recorded with Rick Hall at FAME in Muscle Shoals—"Down along the Cove" was one of them; "Bad News" was the other. Frank Fenter suggested the name of the album, which is also the name of an evil police force in Haiti, fitting perfectly with the album's voodoo theme.

Another of the artists I had the opportunity of working with at Capricorn was Alex Taylor, the brother of James and Livingston Taylor. In 1972, Steve McQueen was doing a movie called *Junior Bonner*. The movie producer was in Tower Records out in Los Angeles—they used to play new records in the store when they were released—when he heard Alex Taylor's record that had just been released on Capricorn. He loved Alex's voice and decided that Alex's voice was perfect to sing a song in the new movie. He went straight to the store manager to ask who was singing, got all the information, bought the record, and took it home. Then he contacted Phil Walden. They hired Alex to fly out there and go into the studio to record this song. It was either later that day or the next that Alex dropped by the Troubadour for a beer. The place was almost empty that afternoon. Only two people sat at a table: Steve McQueen and Ali McGraw. What a coincidence. Alex thought it was a great time to make his acquaintance. He walked over to the table, stuck out his hand, and said, "Hi, Steve. I'm Alex Taylor. I just got finished recording that song for your movie." Steve didn't take his hand. He just looked up at Alex and said, "Oh yeah? Well, kiss my ass!" I asked Alex what he said in return. "I think I said, 'thank you' as I was backing away." McQueen wasn't impressed by Alex. I think it might have been bad timing.

I usually say that Eric Quincy Tate was the first act I produced. I did one before that—Sundown—but I was nervous and didn't know what I was doing back then. It didn't turn out well, so I don't count it. When people ask what the first record I produced was, I say Eric Quincy Tate, *Drinking Man's Friend*, in 1972.

Songwriter and producer Tony Joe White had brought this band, Eric Quincy Tate, in from Texas. He wanted Phil to hear them. Donnie McCormick was the lead singer and drummer; David Cantonwine was the bass player; Tommy Carlisle and later Wayne "Bear" Sauls played guitars, and Joe Rogers played keyboards. I think they cut a few things with Tony Joe that were never released. Phil decided to sign Eric Quincy Tate on Tony Joe's recommendation because Phil had just started managing him (White had a hit with his song "Rainy Night in Georgia," recorded by Brook Benton), and it fell right to me to produce *Drinking Man's Friend*. I liked EQT a lot; their singer, Donnie McCormick, was a superstar. He was so good.

Eric Quincy Tate played at Grant's Lounge in Macon more than any other band; they were practically the house band. The original stage at Grant's Lounge was along the wall on the right when you walk in, to the right of the current stage. It was a small place. The room where the pool tables are now was added later, so you can imagine. There was no upstairs room either.

When we first came to Macon, Grant's Lounge was the only rock and roll club in town. There was an R&B club that was part of the Chitlin' Circuit called Adams Lounge. It was out in Jones county. There might have been one or two country and western nightclubs. At that time, everything was separated. You had a rock club or a country music club. It wasn't all inclusive like it later became. Grant's just happened to be the one that was in downtown Macon and convenient, so all these players, mostly White acts, just started showing up and playing. Many of the bands went there to showcase. It was only a couple of blocks from the studio and office, and they could just walk over. White Witch showcased there, and I remember the night the Tucker band showcased. There were nights when you could see a pile of the best Capricorn artists all jamming into the morning hours, and the cover charge might be a dollar or less.

Meanwhile, we were in the studio recording EQT's *Drinking Man's Friend* on an 8-track recorder. It was a challenge. Donnie McCormick was playing drums and singing at the same time, and we were basically recording the band live. We experimented a little bit, but we were all were pretty new. The record came out, and while it didn't sell a ton, it sold a respectable number of copies.

To this day, I think the album holds up well. I can still enjoy listening to it, even after all these years. It wasn't a "hit," but we got great national reviews, including a rave review from *Creem* and *Rolling Stone* writer Lester Bangs, who also gave a fantastic review to the Marshall Tucker Band on their first album and wrote a very entertaining and positive piece on Wet Willie. Having somebody brag about a project I was involved in meant more to me than actual sales. I never read a bad review of *Drinking Man's Friend*. It was spoken highly of—critically acclaimed, as they say. I thought "maybe I'm onto something here." It was the thing that made me want to be a record producer.

After *Drinking Man's Friend*, EQT was in a perfect position. They could have been as big as the Marshall Tucker Band; all they had to do was come up with another album just as good. The problem was, they just didn't have any songs. All the songs on *Drinking Man's Friend* had been around for years, so they had those down perfectly. We got in there and they tried and tried, but they couldn't match the quality of the songs on the first album.

Wet Willie was one of Capricorn's original breakout bands. Back in Tuscaloosa, I had played in bands with a friend named Frank Friedman. Frank was one of the bass players in South Camp before Charlie Hayward came in. Well, Frank had a band named Wet Willie, and he brought them to Capricorn to try and get them signed. Frank Fenter really liked them, but, for some reason, they ended up not being signed. So that band went nowhere. Some time passed, and Frank found another band down around Mobile, Alabama, called the Fox. He rehearsed them, brought them over, and started calling *them* Wet Willie. Phil took a liking to this version of Wet Willie and signed them, and they became the Wet Willie we all know and love. I cut some of the first demos on them, but I was busy out on the road playing with Alex Taylor, so Frank brought Eddie Offord aboard. He had known Eddie from Great Britain where he had produced the band, Yes. Eddie ended up producing Wet Willie's first album, which was released in 1971.

When it came time for the second album, it fell to me to produce. We cut some demos, but I made a big mistake. We cut a song called "Country Side of Life," and we didn't have the final cut, just a demo. With a lot of work yet to do, Phil called and wanted to hear what we had so far. So, I sent him the rough cut. He heard it and didn't like it, so he gave the project to Johnny Sandlin. I figured Phil could hear through the arrangement and imagine what it would sound like. I'll never forget the wise words I got from Frank Fenter. "Don't ever let anybody hear anything before it's to the point of the best it will ever be," he said. "Everybody is not a producer. Everybody can't see through to what it's going to be like, they only know what they are hearing right there." I shot myself in the foot on that one. I did end up producing *The Wetter the Better* in 1976 and *Left Coast Live* in 1977.

Producing live is quite different than in a studio. In the studio, you're growing it from a seed. You actually *do* produce it. With a live album, there's not a whole lot of producing you can do. You just make sure it's recorded well and engineered well and that the mixing is good. And you might be sure you pick the best songs that were recorded to put on the record. You mostly just take charge.

In 1973, Gregg Allman recorded *Laid Back* at Capricorn. It was his first solo album and featured several ballads, including retelling of two previous ABB tunes, "Midnight Rider" and "Please Call Home." According to Scott Freeman in *Midnight Riders*, "An old R&B song recorded by Rufus Thomas, 'Don't Mess Up a Good Thing,' is the album's break from the ballads. It is a jumping tune full of keyboards with Chuck Leavell on acoustic piano, Gregg on organ and Paul Hornsby on the clarinet." So, I got credit for playing a *clarinet* on a song on *Laid Back*. The original pressings also credited me as playing clarinet, but it was later corrected to *clavinet*.

I continued to play on various records that came out of Capricorn in the mid-1970s, and I got to produce an album on Bobby Whitlock from Derek and the Dominos. The album was called *Rock Your Socks Off* (1976). Unfortunately, Capricorn did little to promote that album. It deserved more attention than it got, but, for some reason, the label never got behind it. Bobby is a great songwriter and singer. My vision cutting that album was to make it sound like a "Layla" record—I wanted it to sound like a band. I wanted the players to work it up live so that it wouldn't sound like he sat down with an acoustic guitar and then we added all this stuff behind him. I brought Les Dudek in from Florida. I like Les, he's a good friend of mine and I like the way he plays guitar, but it just didn't work out. So, Les was out and Jimmy Nalls stepped in. He was glad to be there and only had to go over it a time or two before he had it. I thought the record turned out well. It had a live feel. My favorite cut was "Why Does Love Have to Be So Sad?" that he recorded with the Dominos. I had a band back in the early 1990s called Coupe Deville, and that was one of the first songs we worked up. Bobby had a world of talent and was a great singer, player, and writer. We were good friends. His daughter was born around the time he came here, and my daughter was the same age. They had their birthday parties together and hung out a lot, so our two families spent a lot of time together. Unfortunately, we only got to do that one LP together. He moved back to Memphis shortly after that record. There were some great guests on that album: Dru Lombar, Jimmy Nalls, Rick Hirsch, Jimmy Hall, Chuck Leavell, and more. The nucleus of the project was Kenny Tibbets on bass, Jerome Thomas on drums, Bobby on keys, and Jimmy Nalls on guitar. Everyone else was added as guest spots, after the fact. This became common practice for the records we were doing then. Everyone's album was sort of a family reunion. All the Southern musicians enjoyed a camaraderie.

When Jimmy Carter was governor of Georgia (1970–1975), he and Phil became close friends, and Phil helped Carter's campaign for president by hosting fundraisers, concerts that usually featured the Allman Brothers and Marshall Tucker. I met Carter when Phil brought him to the studio once (he was still governor), but I never had a chance to interact with him much. Phil whispered to me, "You're probably looking at the next president of the United States." It was a great photo op, and they took pictures of him at the board with headphones on. He came to at least one or two of the Capricorn picnics, but by then he was president and you couldn't get anywhere near him for all the security. To this day, if I had a chance to sit down with him, I wouldn't even want to talk about politics. I'd want to talk about his extensive arrowhead collection. I remember in his early days he talked about picking up all these arrowheads on his farm in Plains.

Capricorn's annual picnics became quite popular. Besides us employees, all sorts of celebrities would show up, from Cher to Andy Warhol. At first, they were held at Lake Sinclair. I think the last one they had was at Lakeside, which was an old amusement park that Phil had bought. Oddly enough, my clearest memory of the picnics was playing ping pong with Hank Williams, Jr. I believe at the time Phil was talking to Hank Jr. about signing him to the label. Phil was also talking to me about producing Hank. He was trying to put us together, so Phil kind of steered us together and we ended up playing ping pong. This was around 1974 or 1976, and at that time I played ping pong like my manhood was at stake. I loved some ping pong! I mean, I could tear up a ping pong table. Now, I don't know what made Hank think he could play. We got to playing, and he never got a point. I don't remember how many rounds we played, but it pissed him off, because, you know, Hank thinks pretty highly of himself. I don't know if that sabotaged our working together or not, but I could tell that he was deeply agitated. It was right after that, that he went out on that hunting trip to Montana and fell off Ajax Peak. But we never got together. That game was the last time I ever saw him, but he went on to record "Can't You See," and it really started taking off, which was good for Toy Caldwell. Everybody, from Hank to Waylon, recorded it later.

Photo Album

Paul Hornsby, early farming days, Coffee County, Alabama, 1945.

Piano recital and remembering why I hated piano lessons! Paul Hornsby, front row, third from left. New Brockton Elementary School, ca. 1955.

The Barons, Paul's first band: John Gunder, Chuck Beavers,
Johnny Hass, and Paul Hornsby, 1962.

The Five Men-Its: Left to right: Paul Hornsby, Johnny Sandlin, Eddie Hinton, Fred Styles, and Johnny Campbell, 1965.

THE MINUTES

The Minutes. Just starting out on the road, Nashville, Tennessee, 1966. No matter the spelling, it never made me like the band name. Left to right: Eddie Hinton, Paul Hornsby, Johnny Sandlin, and Mabron McKinney.

First Hour Glass photo in Boutwell Studio, Birmingham, Alabama, 1967.

Hour Glass recording first album in Hollywood, California, 1967.
Left to right: Duane Allman, Gregg Allman, Johnny Sandlin,
Mabron McKinney, and Paul Hornsby.

Hour Glass, 1967. Note Gregg's cane he had to use following the gunshot wound to his foot on the eve of his draft physical.

Lost in Space with Paul Hornsby, Angela Cartwright, Bill Mumy, and Gregg Allman, 1967. *Courtesy Joel Sussman*

Hour Glass performing on the *Upbeat* television show, Cleveland, Ohio, 1968. Left to right: Duane Allman, Gregg Allman, Johnny Sandlin, Pete Carr, and Paul Hornsby.

Recording The Marshall Tucker Band's first album at Capricorn Studio, 1973.

Paul Hornsby, Ovie Sparks, and Charlie Daniels at the mixing board, Capricorn Studio, 1974. *Courtesy Herb Kossover*

Paul Hornsby with Charlie Daniels, visited by Chip Carter, 1975.
Courtesy Herb Kossover

Paul Hornsby (center) with The Marshall Tucker Band showing off
their Gold Record for "A New Life," 1974.

Paul Hornsby producing Charlie Daniels and Toy Caldwell in Nashville, Tennessee, studio, 1989.

Paul Hornsby and Bobby Whitlock at Capricorn Studio, 1975.
Courtesy Herb Kossover

Alabama Urban Cowboy at Gilley's, Pasadena, Texas, 1982.
Courtesy J. Carol Anderson Photography

Paul Hornsby at Capricorn Studio, 1977.
Courtesy Herb Kossover

Paul Hornsby, Coupe Deville days, circa 1990.
Courtesy Joe Davies

Edd and Paul Hornsby, porch pickin', 2002.

The Capricorn Rhythm Section. Back, left to right: Paul Hornsby, Lee Roy Parnell, and Bill Stewart. Front, left to right: Tommy Talton, Scott Boyer, and Johnny Sandlin, 2005. *Courtesy Anne Sandlin*

Capricorn Rhythm Section at the Armory Ballroom, Macon, Georgia, 2006. *Courtesy Bill Thames Photography*

Paul Hornsby is inducted into the Alabama Music Hall of Fame, 2010.
Chuck Leavell in background.

"Older" Paul standing in front of young Paul Hornsby mural,
Dothan, Alabama, 2010.

Paul's mother, Magdalene Hornsby, and Paul at "Paul Hornsby Day," New Brockton, Alabama, 2010.

Paul Hornsby and his children, Lee, April, and Jesse, 2012.

Paul Hornsby and Chuck Leavell throwing a spear using an *atlatl*, ca. 2015.
Courtesy L. Willett

Paul Hornsby in the front office of Muscadine Studios, 2010.
Courtesy Maryann Bates

Paul Hornsby at Muscadine Studios, ca. 2017.
Courtesy J. Carol Anderson Photography

Paul Hornsby with Kunio Kishida and Bill Stewart
at The Big House Museum, Macon, Georgia, 2015.

7

Searchin' for a Rainbow

Shortly after the Wet Willie Band was signed to Capricorn, they played with a band in Spartanburg, South Carolina, that really impressed them. They came back and told Walden about them and an audition gig for the Marshall Tucker Band was set up at Grant's Lounge. Phil liked what he heard, and a demo session was set up. They had previously cut some demos in Muscle Shoals, but nothing had come of that. When you saw them on stage, they presented a freight train full of energy and excitement. There had to be some way to get this across on studio tape.

Not long after the Sundown album, Capricorn signed them. Phil Walden believed in the band from the get-go. He truly saw something in the group. Johnny Sandlin and I were the two staff producers at Capricorn, and Phil handed them off to Johnny and told him to take them into the studio and see what he could do with them. Johnny was hesitant to produce the band because he was busy with the Allmans and other projects, and their country undertones were not his thing. Nothing ever came of the tapes they made with Johnny, and I never heard them.

They handed the Tucker band off to me, and I took it as a challenge. I said, "I have got to make something of this." Now, I'm the type of producer who doesn't want to hear what somebody else has done with an artist. If I'm to produce them, I want it to be my ideas for better or worse, with no other influence. For eight weeks, we lived in the studio and worked fifteen-hour days. When we finally came out and turned in the mixes, I couldn't even hear it anymore, I'd been so close to it.

The Marshall Tucker Band, like the Allmans, was led by two brothers. Toy Caldwell was the primary songwriter and smoking-hot lead guitarist, while Tommy was bassist and the band leader. It was Tommy who addressed the audiences during the show and pretty much kept the show rolling along at maximum velocity. Rounding out the band was George McCorkle, also a songwriter and a fine rhythm guitarist; Paul T. Riddle, the group's youngest member on drums; Jerry Eubanks on flute and saxophone; and lead vocalist Doug Gray. People often ask me about Toy Caldwell. Ol' Toy didn't enter a room—he crashed into it. Bigger than and full of life, Toy wasn't complicated, but he was far from simple, a real son of the South and a hilarious individual. I miss him every day.

I suppose my favorite Tucker memories were from working on that first album. At that time, they had not become a touring band. Most of the members had day jobs. I remember Toy Caldwell driving the four hours from South Carolina down to Macon, playing on the sessions, after having worked all day at his plumber's job. They had that fresh, youthful eagerness about them at that time and were glad to just get the chance to do something in the music world. We were all pretty hungry then. I had not yet proven myself as a producer, and the band's sound was not as defined as it later was. We had more room to experiment in the studio. The album was fresh and different, and I'm not sure that Capricorn Records knew what to do with it. They held on to it for a while. Finally, after the band started opening shows for the Allman Brothers, they were getting noticed, and the fans loved them. Capricorn decided it was time to take a chance and release *The Marshall Tucker Band*.

The rest, as they say, is history. When that thing came out, it just blew everything else out of the water. I went on to produce the next five Marshall Tucker LP's for Capricorn. Besides producing, I played piano on the albums as well, playing on hits that include "Heard It in a Love Song," "Can't You See," "This Ol' Cowboy," and others.

The self-titled album immediately got great reviews, and from the combined exposure the band had gotten from touring with the Allmans, the momentum made the record take off. I think I was as surprised as the band was when the record became a hit. This was my first hit and I can't begin to tell you what a feeling that is! It's like striking the mother lode after many years of dry prospecting!

Lester Bangs of *Rolling Stone* wrote "a moving piece of work that bids to put them in the same league as the Allmans damned fast." Comparisons were being made daily, often calling Tucker "the country version of the Allman Brothers band."

When the Tuckers first came in, they had a whole career worth of songs ready. They had been writing and playing for quite some time. All we had to do was record them, add a few things, and spice it up to do that first album. Then it was a hit, and the sooner an album is a hit, the quicker the label wants another album to follow up on it. They put them out on the road playing every night, and before a year was up, they were back in the studio. You are booked in the studio for three or four weeks, and you can't just come up with twelve brand new tunes ready to go. You can't snap your fingers and get that. The way the Tuckers were, their music became very experimental.

I was always a nervous wreck at the beginning of each of their new albums. You're only as good as your last record, and the pressure to equal or surpass the latest album was great. Toy would come in, and I'd ask, "Toy, do you have any new songs?" He'd say, "Oh, I got some ideas I've been kicking around." We'd go in the studio the next day, and the rest of the band hadn't heard these songs, really. They might have heard Toy thumping around on an acoustic guitar in the dressing room or something. But Toy would start playing on the acoustic, and Paul would fall in on the drums with Tommy on the bass, and we'd get something like that down. Then we'd take off the acoustic and add an electric guitar. We might add another acoustic. We'd just add and take away until it felt right. The last thing was Doug doing vocals, and he'd be in the vocal booth listening to Toy singing through one side of the headphones while he sang his part. It was just a quick way to learn the song. It was experimental and a cool thing, but that became their sound, and they made the most of it. That's how all their records were done except the first one. Of course, we had some experimentation on the first album too. Moog synthesizers had just come out, and I thought it might sound good on "Take the Highway." Nobody told me not to do it. If I had it to do over today, I probably wouldn't do it, but I thought it was a new sound and something I wanted to play with.

Their first album, *The Marshall Tucker Band*, was my third attempt at producing a record. The first was a failure; the second was more promising, so this one had to be the one. As far as having a scientific approach, I had none, and I had little producing experience to draw from. What we had going for us were some great songs that Toy Caldwell had written and a band who were the easiest to work with I had ever met. They brought their enthusiasm with them and played their asses off. Not much thought was given for an "image." We took each song individually and added whatever we thought fit that particular cut. On "Hillbilly Band," we added a fiddle. Toy played steel guitar on several cuts. Wherever there was a "crack" left, I filled it with a keyboard. Everyone got to explore their ideas and try what they wanted. I don't think we left one spot open for anything.

We had a two-inch, MCI 16-track, which was the first big recorder we cut their first album on. That machine was notorious for spilling tape. You'd be rewinding and hit the brakes on the damned thing and sometimes it wouldn't stop. One night we had spent many, many hours on the long jam of Toy's guitar solo on a section of "Take the Highway." We were rewinding the tape, and I hit stop. One of the reels kept going and it spilled tape all over the room. We panicked and started rewinding that thing by hand. There was a section of the tape that had gotten crinkled and we couldn't use it. It was part of the solo, of all places, and could not be replaced. We ended up having to cut four bars out of the solo. We had to cut enough so that it made sense musically. When that machine was moved from the studio it had cowboy boot prints all over it, and most of them were mine! I kicked that machine like a dog.

I had never been involved in the mastering process. But when we did the Tuckers' first album, I physically took it to the mastering lab in New York City, and a guy named George Marino mastered it while I stood there and watched the process. Because I had never seen it done, I always wondered why you had to have it mastered. After all, we had it on the tape. What I didn't understand was that you can only get so much volume on the side of a vinyl record—the longer the playing time on a given side, the less volume you could get. If you had a forty-minute record, it wasn't going to be very loud. Thirty-five minutes was perfect. The louder the music, the broader the groove has to be, but the grooves in a record can be only so wide. And there's just so much space on the side of a record for so many grooves. That also means that the louder the music is, the less fidelity you will have.

If you have a vinyl record of a symphony, that music is usually softer, and you get more time on a record than with a loud rock and roll recording because the grooves don't have to expand as much to compensate for the volume. That's why a 45 is so much louder than an album; with only one song on a side, there's a lot more room. Another thing that a lot of people didn't realize was that the fidelity wasn't as good on the last song on the side of an album. The further you go toward the center hole, the less high end you have, so that's one detail you can compensate for in mastering. With the last song on the side of an album, you might want to add more top end, EQ-wise. When you're recording the album, you don't know what the final sequence of the songs will be, but by the time it goes to the mastering lab, you have the sequence worked out. They can master it accordingly and add more top end.

With CDs, you don't have those problems, but you have other problems. Everybody wants as much volume as they can get. And if you think the LP will be played on the radio, you want that volume because the louder it is, the further that signal can be broadcast. The further the signal reaches, the more ads you can sell because you can tell advertisers "our signal reaches into the next county" or things like that. If you pick out ten rock and roll CDs today, they are going to pretty much be the same volume, whether they're an hour long or twenty minutes, but it didn't work that way with analog recording onto vinyl.

But back to the Marshall Tucker Band. When that first album came out, I was as surprised as anybody. It was the first hit album I had ever worked on. They got put on tour immediately, opening for the Allman Brothers Band, so that was the best audience in the world. Had they not done that, who knows what may have happened? It's all about exposure.

If you don't have exposure, nobody's gonna know about it. And that early version of that band, when they came out on-stage with all that energy, it was just infectious. The audience could feel it. It looked like the band was having the time of their lives, and I think they were having a ball playing that good music. Then everybody went out and bought the album.

Not long after that, they became friends with Charlie Daniels. Toy came in for their second album and told me Charlie was going to play on it. All I knew about him was the novelty hit "Uneasy Rider." I think Charlie's previous album (*Way Down Yonder*) sold around 17,000. Being on the road with a six-piece band, 17,000 copies wasn't much, considering their overhead. The piddly royalty rate they got out of it wasn't much either. But Charlie came in and played fiddle on "24 Hours at a Time," and, by the time we cut the third album, Charlie approached me about doing his new record. I said, "Hell yeah, let's do it now!" By then, Southern rock had become a new musical genre, accepted and loved the world over. It had been a long road since that pioneering Southern rock band the Hour Glass set out for California in 1967.

For the third Tucker album, we did a two-record set called *Where We All Belong* (1974). The Band had wanted to do a live record next, but they had some new songs that really needed to be produced in the studio. So, I suggested we do a live disc and a studio disc. I had to convince some people that it was a good idea, but to me it, live or studio, it was all music. And it worked. Of course, "This Ol' Cowboy" was a single from that one. To me, that's the most fun Tucker song to play live. I love playing that with Chris Hicks. We have a great time, and you can just jam on that thing forever. We had Charlie Daniels (on fiddle) and Andy Stein (who played fiddle with Commander Cody and His Lost Planet Airmen) playing on it. The Cody band was doing a lot of dates with those two bands back then. Rather than record each separately, we had Charlie and Andy set up face to face in the studio, dueling it out. I think both guys played some of their best licks trading off on that song. Andy went on to play in the house band for *A Prairie Home Companion*.

When the Marshall Tucker Band first came into the studio, they insisted that I play piano on their album. Knowing how to play is important when producing; you must be able to communicate with the musicians on their level. As a musician, I've worked with at least a couple of producers who couldn't play a note. I didn't have as much respect for them.

With the Tuckers, I was a bit hesitant at first. I really didn't want to get in there and get in their way. They pretty much twisted my arm to get me to play, so when it came time to do the second album, I was thinking, "If it ain't broke, don't fix it." Since the formula worked the first time, we did it again and I continued to play like that. Everything I played on with them was a hit, and that was the goal of the whole thing. We were really working it and did about two records a year. Capricorn was pushing us to do a new record every nine months. With the first album, they had all those songs ready and had been playing them forever. Then they were playing on the road, and Capricorn wanted a new record. I was used to artists writing and going out and playing the tunes and woodshedding and kicking them around a bit before recording.

We had a small set of speakers sitting on the console at Capricorn, and I always liked listening to the mix through those instead of the big speakers. I thought that was more like what people had in their home or car. Toy always called those the "Fox Drive-in" speakers. He'd say, "play it on the Fox Drive-in!" It reminded him of the little speakers at the drive-in theater that you hung in your car. I mixed their whole first album through those speakers.

The last studio album I did with Marshall Tucker was their biggest, *Carolina Dreams*. We were just finishing that up when we went over to Europe. It was recorded in 1976 but didn't come out until 1977.

Marshall Tucker went to Europe in 1976 with Grinderswitch and Bonnie Bramlett. They played a few dates on the tour before I joined them in London to record. We played Manchester and Birmingham and then we went up to Glasgow, Scotland. We recorded every set every night, and then I came back and put it all together in the studio. As fate would have it, the live album, *Stompin' Room Only*, would not be released until 2003. It was the last album I recorded with the Tuckers. Interestingly, the liner notes booklet was written by my co-author, Michael Buffalo Smith.

We recorded Grinderswitch and Bonnie Bramlett on that European tour also, but I don't think those songs were ever released other than one cut from each on the *Hotels,*

Motels and Road Shows LP (1978), which also had live cuts from other Capricorn artists.

In 1973, Don Kirshner brought his famed *Rock Concert* television show to Macon. The special edition was dubbed "Saturday Night in Macon, Georgia" and featured the All-man Brothers, Marshall Tucker, Wet Willie, and Martin Mull.

I was there helping record the Tucker portion of that. Toy was sick and had a fever of 103. You can tell looking at the photos and film just how sick he was, but they were troopers. While the show helped break out the Tuckers, it didn't do the Allmans much good because they were fussing and fighting. At the time, I remember Wet Willie playing outdoors. They were decked out and giving it everything they had.

Something I might comment on was the attempt to get a hit single out of the Marshall Tucker Band. We would always get a pep talk from Phil Walden; the label wanted us to turn out a hit single, but everything the Tuckers did was ten minutes long. They were a jam band. The record label wanted a version that the radio would play, so we needed to cut those songs in half—at least. No mean feat! I got a lot of practice with razor blades—cutting tape; trying to get a verse, a chorus, a bit of guitar work; finishing off with the chorus, then fade—all within the constraints of three and a half minutes.

It came time to do the *Carolina Dreams* album in 1976, and they didn't have anything ready. We were backstage in Atlanta for Georgia Jam; Toy was picking and Tommy was fooling around on the bass. We were supposed to begin a new album soon.

"Toy," I asked, "how's it looking for material for the new album?"

"Well, I have this one thing here," he said. He started strumming it and singing it, and some of the others were singing along. It was "Heard It in a Love Song." I thought, if we're ever gonna have a hit, that's the one right there. From that moment, we approached that song as a single. We purposely kept it short, with just the required guitar, flute, piano licks added. This was such a melodic song, and I wanted every note, whether played or sung, to stick in every listener's head. From the opening flute lines to the final guitar licks, I think everybody who was around to hear music in the '70s can hum it.

I'll never forget the day we handed in the complete album. The powers that be called me up and said, "What do you think about taking the guys back into the studio to cut a single?"

"Are you shitting me?" I said. "What do you think 'Heard It in a Love Song' is?"

"Well, it might work. I don't know."

"Man, you're crazy," I said. "No, we're not going to cut anything else." Of course, it became their biggest hit. Every time you turned on the radio in summer 1977, you'd hear it. And that was indeed the band's biggest selling record. It went to No. 10 on the pop charts in *Billboard* magazine.

Out of all the cuts I ever played on, I have had more comments on the piano solo in "Love Song" than in all the others combined. There was nothing fancy about it. I just played the basics, just what I could get by with to fill it in. I always say I felt like I was a "fill in" piano player, just filling in the cracks where their records were concerned. But I have had so many compliments on that song.

People have asked me in the past about working in the studio with a band, say, for instance, Marshall Tucker. There are six guys, each with his own opinion, plus me as producer. Somebody has to make the final call on a certain song or sound or other issue. I always listen to each person's opinion—if somebody wants to say something, I welcome it. I may not agree with an idea, but I listen to them. Ultimately, somebody has to assemble all those ideas, of course, taking my own ideas into account as well. It was always difficult when an inexperienced band that had never recorded would come in, but these days recording has become so accessible that you'd be hard pressed to find a band that hasn't recorded something, even just in their own bedroom with a computer and a mike. But in those days, a recording studio was a pretty strange environment. There just weren't that many around. You had to have the producer and engineer to show musicians how to set up, what settings to use, and how much distortion you could live with. There were so many who had never even heard themselves played back on tape.

These days I can blink my eyes, and another year has passed. But what I remember about those days is just how much could happen for a band in a single year. Back when I was with the Five Minutes, we had a six-month period in which we broke up, joined up with the Allman boys, formed the Hour Glass, went to St. Louis, got discovered, and wound up in California with a record deal. That's a lot of ground to cover in such a short time, but when you are twenty-one or twenty-two years old, six months feels like six years.

We were all in and out of the studio in those days. There was nothing else to do other than go fishing, so people were always ending up playing on other folks' albums. It was like inviting someone in for a cup of coffee at your house. "Hey, you wanna come in and pick on our album?" I remember one day Jaimoe came through. We wouldn't usually invite somebody to sit in on the drum kit because we already had Paul Riddle. But for Jaimoe, the obvious thing on "Can't You See" was to add some congas to it. Jaimoe played on various projects; I think he played on a Grinderswitch album, and he played on a Charlie Daniels record. But that day the congas weren't in the studio. Someone might have taken them out to do a gig. So, we just flipped over an acoustic guitar and let him play on the back of that, which is what you hear on "Can't You See." On the liner notes they called it "guitcongas."

Dickey Betts played a lead run on "Searchin' for a Rainbow" (*Searchin' for a Rainbow*, 1975). He always had that unique style, and you could always tell it was him. He played on a Grinderswitch album, too. I remember playing on an Elvin Bishop album, and I also played some insignificant part on a Captain Beyond album and ended up listed on the credits. To this day, I can't remember what I did. There are still a lot of Captain Beyond fans, and sometimes they contact me. I can't believe it. People will ask, "What was it like playing with Captain Beyond?" I just have to say, "I don't remember!" But it was a musically incestuous environment around here back then.

94

8

Capricorn Rising

Capricorn was going through a lot of changes around 1974 and was looking to expand into country music. At that time, everything they touched turned to gold, and every record company of any size had a country division. They ended up signing the "Queen of Country Music," Kitty Wells, to do an album. She was an older artist and "stone country." I had heard her on the Grand Ole Opry when I was a kid. What better way to kick off the country division? This was before the days of female country mega-stars like Shania Twain and Faith Hill, so she seemed like a good first signing. Kitty had not had a hit for some time, and we had never produced a truly country artist before. It was sort of like, "Let's see what we can get away with here—just how progressive can we take her?"

Phil gave the project to Sandlin, but Johnny was no fan of pure country music. I liked some of it because I'd grown up with it, so Johnny asked me if I would co-produce the album. My music needs to have a little syncopation in it, so I was never was a fan of hardcore country music, but I took it on as a challenge. I also did it for my mother and daddy because I knew they'd be proud. I think there was a lot of that going around because nearly all the musicians on Capricorn wanted to play on the album—and did. Aside from myself, contributing players and singers included Johnny Sandlin, Scott Boyer, Tommy Talton, Chuck Leavell, Richard Betts, Toy Caldwell, John Hughey, David Brown, Bill Stewart, Donna Hall, Ella Avery, Mary Dorsey, Diane Pfeifer, and Joyce Knight. I wonder just what this older country lady thought when she was thrust into a rock and roll studio full of hippies down in Macon, Georgia. She seemed overwhelmed at first but eventually started to trust our musical instincts.

About halfway into it, Johnny told me, "I just can't take this anymore. Will you take it?" I agreed, and I think we did a good job with it. The songs we brought in were a lot more contemporary than anything she'd done before—if the tempo was syncopated at all, she couldn't feel it. It had to fall on the down beat. We cut stuff like Otis Redding's "I've Been Loving You Too Long" (which I think was the best cut on the LP), Bob Dylan's "Forever Young," which became the album's title, and one of Toy's songs, "Too Stubborn." Scott Boyer was there, and we called him the "stunt singer." He'd lay down a vocal first, so when she was singing, she could hear his voice in the headphones, and that's how we got the vocal performance out of her.

I think she liked the project more than her husband, Johnny Wright, did. He seemed a little skeptical and was a bit difficult. The Otis Redding song on there wasn't quite country to him, and it was ironic that one of the best cuts on the album was "I Been Loving You Too Long." She nailed that, but that was one of the songs her husband objected to. He didn't really want her to stretch too far from what she had always done, and I understood that. I never heard from them after that. I was already on down the road working on another Tucker album.

About twenty years ago, I was leaving to go to Nashville to find a studio to hire Nashville players for a recording I was doing here. I think I was going to record Jimmy Nalls and Randy Howard, the fiddle player (not the singer). They had relocated to Nashville. I was calling around to find what studios had the same tape format that I had. I called one studio and a young guy answered the phone.

"John Sturdevant!" I said. "You must be John Junior because I knew your daddy. I'm Paul Hornsby, and I produced your grandma!" John Sturdevant, Sr. was Kitty Wells's son-in-law. He got excited.

"Oh man! You did that *Forever Young* album! What a great record! That record was ahead of its time," he said. "We've been trying to capture that sound ever since y'all did that." I was happy to hear he liked it.

As big as Capricorn sounds today, it was really a small label. They were always affiliated with larger labels, but they only had so much money they could spend to promote things. The Allmans were their flagship band. They didn't start promoting Marshall Tucker until Tucker had made it on their own. It wasn't until the first Tucker album took off that

Capricorn started spending money on them. You pretty much had to prove what a band was capable of before they'd spend any money. Grinderswitch was a great band and had some good exposure, but they never got pushed and didn't get the money spent on them. It takes a lot of money for the hype and publicity.

At first, Grinderswitch, as I remember, was a side project for Dickey Betts. Some of the members roadied some for the Allman Brothers. They did not have a keyboard player at first, so I remember working up some songs with them in the beginning with me on piano.

When I first got to know Joe Dan Petty and Dru Lombar and them, we used to congregate at the studio at night. It was the place to be, and we'd all jam. Eventually we got several tunes down, and I suggested we record a few and see if we could get Phil Walden's interest. He liked what we played for him and asked to hear what else we could do. So, I had this Wurlitzer electric piano I got from Gregg. I put it in my trunk and went down to their band house in Peach County. We'd jam all night, and we soon came up with enough material for an album. I played piano on it. They were a two-guitar band. After Capricorn heard the tapes, they decided to let us finish the LP. *Honest to Goodness* came out without a lot of fanfare, but it sounded so good that we wound up doing several more. I also played on the second album. I think they hired Steve Miller, a great B-3 player, for keyboards before the third album. From then on, I just produced and engineered their records. I continued to produce them, even after they left Capricorn.

Grinderswitch played some of the finest boogie stuff I had ever heard. They could play a "shuffle" better than anyone, but even after several LPs, the group just never took off. I think of Grinderswitch as the "trench soldiers" of the Capricorn roster. They never got the push a lot of other groups got, but they had heart and never slowed down from touring and gigging. Through all the hard times a group like that endures, they kept a sense of humor and it kept them going. There isn't a day that goes by that I don't think of some hilarious line quoted by their bassist, the late Joe Dan Petty.

One day I came into the studio and Sam Whiteside, the engineer. was in there. Bonnie Bramlett had been working on her duets album, *Lady's Choice.* I asked Sam what they were doing.

"We're waiting for Joe Cocker to come to," he said. "He's in there on the drum riser, passed out drunk." I told Sam I had never seen Joe up close, so I walked out there and looked down at him. I remember saying, "He sure looks natural." I waited around a long time, but Joe never woke up. They said he never sobered up, so they gave up.

Back in 1975, Elvin Bishop came by my house late one night. We were drinking and talking, and my wife and kids were asleep in the other part of the house. Elvin and I were doing a little guitar pull. We had a gut-string guitar leaning against the wall, and I had a Wurlitzer piano in there. He started playing me some songs, and he had a brand new one. He said, "Let me play you this one, old buddy. If you get somebody to cut it, I'll give you the publishing on it." He started playing and singing.

"Man," I said, "that's a hit song if I ever heard one!" I had an old boom box sitting there and I stuck a cassette tape in and said, "Let's run through it again." So, I recorded it. I promised him that if I could find somebody to cut it, I would. I had Marshall Tucker coming up soon and then Charlie Daniels, but I knew it wasn't the right fit for either of them. Well, it took about two months to finish those two albums. Right after that, I was listening to the radio in my car and this song came on that I recognized. It was that song we had stayed up all night playing. I thought, "Wait a minute, that ain't Elvin singing." It was Mickey Thomas, and the song was "Fooled around and Fell in Love." I found that cassette a couple or three years ago. I have it in the studio, and recently played it for some folks. They thought it was the coolest thing.

Potliquor sent a demo in and it caught Phil's attention right off the bat. He thought the band could be "a new Little Feat" and wanted to do a 45. So, we cut two songs on them in 1977. Part of the band was good, but part wasn't. They never got any more material as strong as the single. They had done an album in 1973, but I don't know what label it was on. I later went down to Baton Rouge to record some new songs, but by then they had lost some band members and I just didn't feel it.

Two Guns, I believe, was the last act to come out on Capricorn before they closed. They were brought in from Oklahoma by Phil Walden's brother, Alan. They were a hot band with two flashy guitar players, hence the name. With the label going under, the record didn't have much of a chance for promotion. Interest soon dropped, and the band never took off. I think they could have gone further if it hadn't been for bad timing on the label's part.

When Phil Walden first hired our rhythm section, it was a weekly salary, and we were expected to play on whatever sessions came in. Whether it was one session a week or 1,000, we still got $175 a week. He also promised a percentage on whatever we played on, and there would be an established percentage pool. He said that was how the Muscle Shoals guys were set up. If that's true, they must have been rolling in dough, because they just had hit after hit. We all thought that sounded great. So, the first album we cut, the self-titled *Livingston Taylor* album (1970), was a hit. We went to Phil, but he said, "I can't give you a percentage on that one. I'm not making any money." Capricorn wasn't yet established. It was Atco records with a stamp that said "Capricorn Series." We grumbled, but we stayed on.

After all the time we were there, we never got paid from a production pool. All we got was that weekly check. Finally, after it went on for a while, I went in and talked to Johnny and Pete, and they were grumbling too.

"Let's quit grumbling about this shit," I said, "and go in and talk to him." They thought he might fire us, but I said, "I don't give a shit. Follow me, guys." We went en masse to his office and told him we just couldn't do this anymore. He had also promised us a raise after a few months, but that time had come and gone...no raise. We walked out of there with a fifty-dollar-a-week raise. That helped immensely and kept us on. But it was that kind of thing all the time. Then he had promised Johnny and me a certain percentage of royalties on albums we produced. After the first Marshall Tucker album became a hit, he handed me a check. I asked him how it was figured and what it was based on. He told me not to worry about it—"it's fair." I still wanted to know how he figured what to pay me, but he never would say. Here we are, the album goes gold, and I'm still getting $175 a week. He gave me a few dollars, but it wasn't enough to pay for a gold record.

The next year we did the second MTB record. I was a known record producer but still didn't have a contract. All I had was, "Don't worry about it. It's fair." So, I got a New York lawyer, and we got to talking. He told me I was getting screwed, but I didn't need to pay someone a hundred dollars an hour to tell me that. He got in touch with Phil, but Phil stopped taking his calls. We finally got something, but it wasn't nearly as much as other producers were getting who had hits.

Phil never would put a deal in writing, so in summer 1974, I set up a meeting through Phil's secretary, Carolyn Brown, to come in and discuss it. I got there, and his door was closed. I told Carolyn I was there to see Phil, but she said, "He told me to tell you there will be no negotiations."

"Well, Carolyn," I said, "it's been good knowing you. Love you. But this is goodbye." I went around the corner to Frank Fenter's office, took my studio key off the keyring, and laid it on his desk.

"What's this all about?" he asked.

"I just can't stay here any longer."

"Oh, don't do that," he said. "Don't leave." I told him to go around to Phil's office, unlock the door, and tell him I am here to negotiate. Otherwise, I was gone.

"You know I can't do that," Frank said. "I can't convince Phil."

The name of the parent company was No Exit, so I told Frank, "I've just found that exit," and I walked out. Oh, Lord, I got to hearing the repercussions from that. He was mad. I don't think anyone had ever quit him. Plus, I had just found out my wife was pregnant, and here I was without a job. I was scared to death and didn't know if I'd ever work again. Well, within a week, I had a call to do the Heartwood project.

Heartwood was on the GRC label in Atlanta. They were a Southern rock band that sounded like the Eagles. That's the first time I met Davis Causey, later a member of Sea Level. They told me they had a friend they wanted to bring in to play some guitar. Davis came in and just blew me away. The label had one big hit, "Chevy Van," by Sammy Johns.

GRC had some bad luck when the owner of the label got into trouble and was sent away. The owner was Michael Thevis, also known as "Mr. T." He just loved me to death. I didn't know anything about his legal situation at first. All I knew was that he had a label, and his A&R men had asked me to listen to a band they had to see if I'd be interested in producing them. I had just left Capricorn and was looking for work. I liked the band a lot, and Thevis would just open his check book to me. He told me to let him know if I needed anything; he put me up in a nice hotel in Atlanta and gave me anything I wanted. I guess they wanted to sign me as a producer. Thevis had so much money, he just bought himself a record label and some artists.

We were recording Heartwood's LP *Nothin' Fancy* in the afternoons at Thevis's studio called the Sound Pit. The day after our first session, a big automobile roared up, and Mr. T got out. He had guys in suits on either side of him.

"Everything the way you like it?" he asked. I told him it was going great.

"Anything you need?"

"No," I said. "It's all good."

"You sounded good last night!" he said. I didn't understand what he meant. I thought he was just making small talk.

The next day at five minutes before three he and the guys in suits were back.

"Everything the way you like it?" he asked again. I told him again it was going great.

"Anything you need?"

"No," I said. "It's all good."

"You sounded good last night!" All I could think to say was "Thank you." When he left, I asked the engineer what he meant because he hadn't been there during the recording sessions.

"Oh," the engineer said, "he's got this place bugged. He can hear every single sound that is made in here from home."

To tell you the truth, it was a little scary. But we got to where we'd be recording and say, "Let's send this one out to Mr. T!" That became our running joke. Thevis ended up with a life sentence in the clinker. The record label folded, but I liked him. He was my buddy.

After the Heartwood project, it came time to do another Tucker record and they stood up for me with Capricorn. They told Phil they didn't want anyone else producing them but Hornsby. I always thanked them for doing that. Walden talked to my lawyer and said that, instead of an exclusive producer contract, we will do contracts for one artist and one record at a time. I guess he thought he was punishing me, but it suited the hell out of me. The first record I did under the contract was Marshall Tucker's *Where We All Belong*. It was a giant record. On the heels of that was Charlie Daniels's *Fire on the Mountain*, the first record not on the Capricorn label. Had I still been in my old situation, I could not have done Charlie's album. I had four records on the charts at one time in 1975. After all that, Phil and I shook hands and were buddies from then. Suddenly, he and I were talking on the phone, not even about the business, but just talking. I guess it took all that for us to become friends. A year later, after Capricorn folded, Phil would call me up and we would just talk. He was a fellow Western movie aficionado like I was, and he even gave me some old movie posters signed by Roy Rogers. He even acted in the Marshall Tucker film for "Long Hard Ride." I was invited to be in it and really wanted to, but I was having spine problems. I could hardly get out of bed, and the doctor was talking about putting me in traction. There was no way I could fly out to Los Angeles and get on a horse.

I decided my family and I needed a vacation, so we went down to Florida. Just as we got to the Florida line, we stopped for a break. I got out of the car and noticed all the tension in my neck and spine was gone. For the first time in months, I could turn my head. I threw away the medications and never had more pain. We stayed in Florida for a month, and when we got back, I was a new man.

Once I became an indie producer, I did projects for labels other than Capricorn. Such was the case with Missouri, a group from Kansas City that had done a self-produced album. It had received some local airplay in their home state, so Polydor hired me to re-cut the record and polish it up. I lost track of them after it came out, and for some reason, not much was heard from them again.

Cooder Brown was a great little band from Texas on Willie Nelson's Lone Star Records label. They were fronted by the great fiddle player Larry Franklin, who later played with Asleep at the Wheel. His fiddle was the lead instrument. They didn't have a lead guitar player, so I called in Jimmy Nalls. We turned that record out pretty quickly, and the life of the label was nearly as quick. I don't know all the business behind the label folding, but there went the career of the band.

The Capricorn years were a great time. There was jamming and recording going on day and night. I got to be friends with Elvin Bishop, and I'm sure I ended up on one or two of his records. We made a lot of music together. Same with Boz Scaggs—he was a jamming buddy. We'd fish in the daytime and end up jamming in the studio at night. That's just the way Capricorn was. It couldn't have been more conducive to making good music. Nobody ever interfered or told us what to do. When I was the studio manager and had a key, I could stay as long as I wanted.

On October 21, 1979, Capricorn filed for bankruptcy. The court action caused a domino effect of lawsuits against Capricorn from bands, artists, and producers because they all lost substantial amounts of money. It had a staff of good people, but when it came down to it, Capricorn was a one-man company, and Phil had gotten distracted by politics at a critical time. After spending much of his time getting Jimmy Carter elected president, Phil then followed him to the White House. I saw it happening, and a lot of the artists were disgruntled because they couldn't get anything done. I heard it straight from them; Phil was their manager, you know? He'd be in Washington where nobody could reach him, and nobody else could make decisions, so it fell apart. Of course, he relaunched the label later, but it wasn't the same, and it failed a second time.

9

Volunteer Jam

On the annual Volunteer Jams staged by Charlie Daniels, I probably would have had more fun just being in the audience listening, or maybe playing on stage. From a producer's standpoint, it was frustrating. During the concerts, I mostly stayed in the remote truck overseeing the taping end. The early Jams were just that—mostly jamming, without a lot of planning. For instance, there would be ten guitar players playing at one time, various singers, keyboards, etc., going full tilt. They were jams in the truest sense of the word. Then came the job of editing the stuff down to try to make an interesting record. I'd have to listen to all these guitar solos happening at the same time and pick the best one.

There was an overwhelming excitement associated with those events, though. We knew some of the artists who were invited to play, but there would always be some big surprises. Part of the very first jam was included as a bonus disc inside the *Fire on the Mountain* LP by the Charlie Daniels Band. As I'm writing this, I'm looking at a version of the album that was originally released on the Kama Sutra label. There was a bonus 45 included and just says "Volunteer Jam" part

1 and part 2. I don't have a 45 RPM turntable handy, or I'd play it and tell you the title of the songs. I think it's just as the title says—a jam. The *Fire on the Mountain* album was originally released on the Kama Sutra label, but it was then re-released on the Epic label. Charlie had then signed with CBS Records, which is now Sony. The bonus disc was not included in the Epic reissue.

10

Going Indie with the Long Haired Country Boy

When I left the position as Capricorn staff producer in the mid 1970s and went independent, I could produce artists on other labels. One such artist was the Charlie Daniels Band. I recorded five albums with Charlie, including the Southern anthems, "The South's Gonna Do It Again" and "Long Haired Country Boy." In addition to the five studio albums, we did three or four Volunteer Jam live albums with practically everyone in the world on stage together, including Willie Nelson. I also continued to produce other acts for Capricorn even though I was no longer employed by the label.

Three months after I left Capricorn, I produced *Fire on the Mountain* in 1974 (No. 38, 1975). It was one of the fastest-recorded albums I have ever worked on. The guys got in there and just did it. It only took twelve days total, including a day of pre-production when they came in and ran over the songs. We recorded and overdubbed for five days, and the rest were mixing. It was released on Kama Sutra and became huge. To this day, that's the biggest record I've ever been involved with. From the cover to the music, it was all just first class. Flournoy Holmes's cover design helped to sell it as much as anything. I still think it's one of the best covers that he ever did.

One memory I have is that the album was almost done, and I realized there wasn't a fiddle song on the record. I was always pushing Charlie to play fiddle. The band had the same lineup as the Allman Brothers Band—two guitars, keyboard, two drummers—and a lot of the music sounded reminiscent of the Brothers, which is good, but I knew there was more there to be had. I had seen Charlie bring the audience to a frenzy in concert playing the fiddle tune "Orange Blossom Special." I mentioned to Charlie that he should use the fiddle more. So, when he came to the studio, he had an instrumental he had been putting together that we temporarily called "Fiddle Boogie." It was a good song, but I just had a feeling that it could be much more. I suggested to Charlie that he consider writing lyrics for the song, and he said he'd give it some thought. Every day after that I asked him about it, and he'd say, "I'm thinking on it."

Finally, we got down to the last day of recording. Well, he went into the other room for a while, maybe thirty minutes, and he came back out with the words on a yellow pad. He said, "Let's try this," and he went to singing about "Lynyrd Skynyrd's pickin' down in Jacksonville" with these words about "people down in Georgia come from near and far to hear Richard Betts playing on that red guitar." The two engineers and I nearly fell out! We were like, "that's it!" So was born, "The South's Gonna Do It Again."

In those days we didn't put out a single, we waited to
see what song the DJ's were going to play from the album
before we pulled a single. It seemed like no time had passed
when I got a call from management in Nashville. "You'll
never believe which song is getting the most play," the manager said. It was "The South's Gonna Do It Again." He said
they are playing the hell out of that at WLS in Chicago.
That became the Charlie Daniels Band's first hit (#29,
1975), soon followed by "Long Haired Country Boy," which
featured guest Dickey Betts on dobro (#56, 1975).

I get another question a lot about the *Fire on the Mountain* because there is no song with that title on the album.
There's an old fiddle song by that name, and it inspired the
name of the LP. Then after *Fire on the Mountain* came out,
George McCorkle from the Marshall Tucker Band was
looking at the great cover art from that album and was inspired to write his song by that title. It's always caused a little
confusion that there's an album by one group and a song with
the same name by another group.

I didn't play a lot on Charlie's albums. He already had a
great piano player in the band named Joel "Taz" DiGregorio.
I may have only played on two or three of his songs at most.
With them, I tried to stay out of the way as much as possible
and be an outside ear. I engineered some, played some, and
helped make the musical decisions. With all the other acts,
it was about the same approach.

As I produced, different acts required somewhat different approaches. With the Marshall Tucker Band, I was sort
of like an extra band member in the studio. Their material

was mostly worked up in the studio. With their excessive touring, they didn't have much time for working up new material. A lot of it started in the studio with just a seed of an idea by Toy Caldwell, the band's lead guitarist and primary song writer. He would have the lyrics and chord changes for the song. He and other band members would sit around the studio, with me on piano, and experiment with ideas until something sounded good on tape. I played keyboards on most of their stuff. On some, I engineered as well. I guess you'd say that I just did anything that was needed to get the job done.

Charlie Daniels, on the other hand, had a different approach. His ideas mostly came together before he hit the studio, so he knew what he wanted when he came in. His style was more as a single artist with the feel of a live band, at least in that he wrote the songs, sang them, and played them from the start. While he wrote all his own material, he credited each band member for their contributions to the arrangements. When somebody is seasoned like Charlie was, it takes a great load off.

One memory of Charlie: We had just finished recording their second album, *Saddle Tramp*, and he had bought a fiddle to use on the record. I think he got it in New York. It wasn't a great fiddle, but he used it on the album. I don't recall if Charlie had met my daddy at this point, but I was always talking to Charlie about my daddy being an old-time fiddle player. Charlie thought that was kind of cool because he knew where that kind of music came from, and it was a part of his heritage too.

The day we finished the album, he handed me that fiddle and said, "Give this to your daddy." It was such a generous gesture. It wasn't a Stradivarius, but it meant a lot to me and to my daddy because it came from Charlie. Down around south Alabama where I come from, Daddy was kind of a local celebrity. He was always talking about that fiddle Charlie had given him, and before long he had people coming out to the house just to see the fiddle that Charlie had given him. One day I went to visit them at the farm, and they had clipped a piece out of the newspaper that described an upcoming event in Enterprise, Alabama. Some group was going to be selling antiques and canned goods and raising money for different charities. Daddy and his cousin were going to play live music. The newspaper said, "Appearing will be Ed Hornsby, James Tindol and Charlie Daniels' fiddle." A few years later I saw Charlie. I hadn't seen him in a while, and I told him, "Charlie, you have truly made it now!" I told him the story and said, "Now you can just stay home and send your fiddle out on tour!" He saw the humor in that.

Marshall Tucker and the Charlie Daniels Band together became a hit package. I truly believe it never got any better than that. It was high-energy Southern fried rock and roll every night.

Randy Richards was from Birmingham. He had two brothers, and their parents, who owned a big discount eye business, were pretty well-to-do. When these guys were teenagers, their parents bought them a 24-track recording studio to play around in. Randy was talented—a good singer and a very prolific songwriter. A lot of people didn't get along with him, but I got along great with him. Randy wanted me to produce an album for him. He had a house in Malibu, so I first went out there to hear his songs and decide which ones to cut. Then we went to his studio in Birmingham. It was called New London. We assembled musicians, using a good many from Capricorn like Bill Stewart and Jimmy Nalls. We cut tracks, then flew back to California to add strings and vocals out there at the Record Plant.

One night while we were out there, Randy and I went to the Troubadour. I was drinking a lot of draft beer. To me, draft beer is not much more than water. I could drink a keg of it before I knew it. Well, I got a little bit lit. It was about midnight when we were heading back to his home in Malibu. We got about a block away from the club, and I said, "Randy, I've got to take a leak. Pull into a station."

"There ain't nothing that's gonna be open at this time of night," he says.

"Are you kidding me?" I said. "We're in Hollywood, California, and there's no place to use the bathroom?"

"Hold on a minute," he said. "I know a little ol' gal that lives up here in an apartment. She'll let you use hers." We walked up the stairs and knocked on the door. Now, I was Marshall Tuckered-out in those days and was wearing my cowboy hat. Randy did a quick introduction and explained that I'd like to use her bathroom. There was a piano near the door, so I reached over and hit a couple of keys just by reflex. Now this woman obviously didn't like Randy, and she took it out on me. She started scolding me, "Don't be playing the piano at this time of night! We have neighbors!" By now I had forgotten about having to pee. Then she took a look at me in my hat and said some smart-ass comment like, "Did you park your horse outside, cowboy?" She kept hurling insults, but what got me was when she asked me if the women back home all still have beehive hairdos.

"Randy," I said, "we better get out of here before I have to kill this bitch." We got back outside under the streetlights of the apartment complex. And I asked, "Does that bitch have a car?"

"Yeah, that little foreign job is her car," he answers. Well, I pulled it out and started hosing down the windshield! I was writing my name with it! I got about half a bladder down when I noticed her window was down on the driver's side. I couldn't believe my luck. I walked around and stuck it in the window and hosed down the inside! Randy was right behind me and warned me I was going to get arrested. Cars were driving by honking their horns, but I just stood there, letting it fly.

A couple or three weeks went by, and we were back in Birmingham. Now, Randy had a gift. He could talk his way into anything he wanted. He had taken up with Dyan Cannon, the actress, and she was flying from L.A. to the studio. Then they were going to drive back across the country in a Rolls Royce he had bought. He didn't want to go by himself, so he talked her into it. Now remember, she was a big star at the time. She had just done *Honeysuckle Rose* with Willie Nelson. Randy introduced us, and she said, "Paul Hornsby?

You're the guy that pissed on the girl's car, aren't you?!" I was caught! She told me she was going to put that scene in one of her movies one day.

The Good Brothers were from Canada. The record market in Canada was minute compared to the USA (and still is). They were with the RCA label in Canada (completely different than our RCA). We recorded two of their albums there in Toronto. They won the Juno award—the equivalent of our Grammy—just about every year that they had one.

Jim Beer & the Rivers' *Turtle Island* was an independent release. He is part Lenape Indian. He walked in Muscadine Studio one day. He had no idea who I was, but we were both wearing shirts with Native American designs. We got to talking more about Indians than music, and then I took a listen to his music—it was tribal oriented but melodic. Often Indian music has a lot of drums with very little melody, but he was a guitar player and very melodic. We cut a CD that featured Chris Hicks on several cuts. It turned out to be one of my favorite albums.

The album I cut on the band Target (*Captured*, 1977) was one of the most stressful ever, but not because of the band. I went to Memphis to hear them rehearse. They were hot. They had two guitars, bass, and drums, but when it came time to go into the studio, one of the guitar players didn't show up. The lead singer, Jimi Jamison, who later became front man for Survivor ("Eye of the Tiger"), was a star just as sure as there was an Elvis. He was always right on the lip. He was known as the singer of the theme song for *Baywatch*. But on this day, they showed up as a trio with a singer. We found out that in the week between rehearsing them in Memphis and recording in Macon, one of the guitar players had had a feud with management and quit the band. They had management problems the whole time they were here, so every day was stressful. The guitar player Dave Cannon who came had to pull double duty, playing on the tracks and then coming back to play the other guitar player's parts. But the band members and I got along great.

11

The All-American Redneck
Who Inspired Muscadine Studios

Muscadine Studios may not have happened had it not been for country singer Randy Howard. Randy was a Macon boy, and he was always playing at this big nightclub here called Whiskey River. He was in the house band and making good money. It was the late 1970s or early '80s, and Capricorn had closed down. It had been the only studio in town, and when they closed, that put a stop to recording in middle Georgia. I was tired at the time anyway, so I took about a three-year break from the business. I ended up getting bored, so I bought an 8-track reel-to-reel tape machine so I could do some recordings of myself and keep my hand in it. I had an office that I turned into a music room.

I knew of Randy Howard, but I had never met him. One day he called me and asked if I could record a demo for him. I knew he played acoustic guitar and sang, so I invited him to come out to see me the next afternoon. I figured he'd bring his guitar, and we'd knock it out. Well, the next afternoon came, and I heard vehicles outside. I looked out to see a station wagon, a van, and a pickup truck all pulling up. People were getting out carrying drums and amps. I panicked. I said, "Wait a minute! I don't have a studio out here. I thought it was just going to be you and a guitar!" He wanted to record the whole band, so I had to think of something quickly to keep them from being disappointed. I had a spare bedroom right off my office, and we moved the bed, set up the drums in the corner, and put one amplifier in the closet and one in the bathroom. I told him I only had two or three mikes, but they had brought all these mikes and cables and plugged everything up.

We got started and were just having a great time. It was the first time I'd recorded anybody in three years. We recorded for about a week and came up with ten or twelve songs. Now, the one song he was known for that everybody wanted to hear was called "All-American Redneck." We cut that one. It was an audience participation song. It went something like, "He drives a pickup truck, he loves to…." Then he'd hold the mike out to the audience, and they'd scream the word that rhymes, like "He pumps gas, he kicks ass," and a few curse words like that. It was always amazing to me that there were more women yelling out the cuss words than men. I guess it was fun for them to use cuss words and get away with it. We recorded the song in the house without having the audience there to yell out the words. We tried having the band yell out the words, but something about having four people doing it was not the same, you have to have at least four hundred to give "F--k" the impact it deserves, so we needed a different idea.

I decided they'd take my quarter track recorder with them to Whiskey River that night and told them to put a mike on the audience and record the song. The next day, we took the audience yelling segments from that tape and added them to our studio recording, making it sound like a live recording. What it lacked in fidelity, it made up for in just pure charm. You could tell by the demo that we were just having a ball. I thought about it for a while and figured we could sell this thing to a label and tell them it's a live record. We might get away with it. So, we did. We sold it to a subsidiary of Warner called Warner/Viva Records and a guy named Snuff Garrett. He had produced Cher and a whole bunch of others. He and Clint Eastwood were partners in this label. Their biggest act at the time was Frizzell and West. This was around 1981 or '82. We sold it to them, and it went to No. 41 in the nation according to *Billboard* magazine. What a kick it was that a bedroom recording with a dubbed-in audience charted like that.

Well, that was all I needed to go out and start looking for a building to open my own studio. I thought, if I can do this in my office, imagine what I could do with a real, freestanding recording studio. The sky would be the limit. So that was then, and now I just celebrated my thirty-seventh year with Muscadine Studio, all because of the inspiration from Randy Howard and that recording.

Unfortunately, the story has a sad ending. Randy had developed a drinking problem and was getting into trouble, driving drunk, driving without a license, that type of thing. He was up at his cabin in Lynchburg, Tennessee, and he got in trouble and went to jail. After so many times, the judges lose their sense of humor about it, and one time they locked him up for about four months. While he was taking a shower in jail, he slipped and broke his femur, the big bone between the hip and knee. It was a bad break, and he spent time in the hospital. He then sued the sheriff's department for not having the right kind of non-skid mats in the shower.

When he was out on probation, he was out driving and had a flat tire. Well, the police who stopped to help him ran his license and found that he was driving on a suspended license. They found a soda straw in his car and called it drug paraphernalia and added a bunch of equally lame charges, so they put him back in jail. Eventually they dropped them all except for driving with a suspended license. He was out on bail again, but he failed to appear in court to answer to that charge because he had fallen again at his house and re-broken his leg. He was in real pitiful shape, hobbling around with a walker. A bounty hunter showed up, banging on his door, and I guess it took him longer to get to the door with the walker than the bounty hunter thought it should take, so he kicked in the door and fired his gun. Randy ducked into his bedroom to get away, but the bounty hunter shot through the wall and hit Randy in the liver. They air-lifted him to the big hospital in Nashville where he died five hours later. The Tennessee Bureau of Investigation initially ruled his killing as murder. Everybody thought charges would be brought against the bounty hunter, but they never were. He was living up there by himself and didn't have any family to go and stand up for him, so nothing was ever done about it. It made the news around the world, and I even did an interview with a reporter from London. The headlines read like he could have written them himself: "Outlaw Country Singer Killed at Tennessee Cabin in Shootout with Bounty Hunter."

As for Muscadine Studio, it is equipped with a lot of vintage gear and instruments that would be at home in a rock museum—50s Telecasters, a B-3 Hammond with the old Hour Glass Leslie tone cabinet (still played every day), Gregg's Wurlitzer piano used on *At Fillmore East*, and on and on. But the fact is, recording is not about the building or the equipment. People get caught up in all that and start to think, "All we have to do is use this or that old studio or this type of recording gear," but it's not about all that. What's important are the people who are running and operating the equipment, the people who work with it. With my studio, I'm not trying to sell folks on the tools I use. I am selling myself, for better or for worse. If you like what I have done, come and get you some more of it. I am digital, but affordable. I record to a hard disc. With a $100 hard drive, you can record multiple albums. It costs less to record this way than it did to record those platinum albums back in the seventies! And the technology is miles ahead of what it was.

It all starts with a good song. Then, it's the presenter of the song—the singer or instrumentalist. Then, it's the engineer/producer who molds it into the best possible performance. Along with that is the equipment used to get the fidelity across. But great recordings can be made with all types of equipment. That's the least important part of the process.

I was recording on reels of tape all the way up until fifteen years ago. I used to get two or three calls a day from people back then who wanted to know if I was digital. That was the buzz word back then. The first digital tapes available to studios were ADAT tapes. They had eight tracks; you could sync up three of those and have twenty-four tracks. But I was still analog and using two-inch tape. At that time, a roll of two-inch tape cost a $150. Fifteen years ago, that was a lot of money. And you could only get sixteen minutes of recording time on a tape, so only two and a half or three songs. So, the tape cost was high, and that's not even considering what the studio time cost. It got expensive quickly. Now, a roll of that tape would be more than $200. Of course, it is rarely used anymore. You could buy three ADAT tapes for a few bucks and have enough tape to do an album, so that caught on quickly. But people would call and ask if I was digital. I would say no—and hear a click when they hung up.

After I got my ADAT machines, and the hard disc recorder, they started flocking in. Then, before I knew it, people were calling and asking, "You're analog, aren't you?" I'd tell them I'm digital; they'd say thank you and hang up. These things go in cycles. I think it's pretty much all ad-driven and what everyone else is doing. That was when "vintage" became the new buzz word. People couldn't wait to embrace digital, and then they wanted analog. That reminds me of record sales back when CDs first came out. That was the quickest format change I had ever witnessed. Within a year all the vinyl was gone, and you couldn't find a turntable for sale. People were just giving them away. I'd like to thank the person who came up with the word "vintage." Before that, I had a studio filled with old, used equipment. Suddenly, that same gear is "vintage." Sounds better, doesn't it? Now, in the past few years, people want to record to vinyl again.

As you can imagine, I record a lot of local acts, but as well, people from all over. One of the great artists I was able to meet through Muscadine was Chris Hicks. Chris was a young hot shot guitar player around town, and when I met him, he was in a band called Loose Change. Alan Walden had found him and brought him into my studio. The band cut quite a bit of stuff in Muscadine Studio, and even after they broke up, Chris continued to cut things in my studio. He would cut his own material as well as work on projects for other people in there. Then I did his record *Dog Eat Dog World* a few years back, and he cut one of my songs, "Georgia Moon," on the album. I've written a few songs, but that one, which I wrote in 1989, is a favorite.

Chris Hicks really did a great job with "Georgia Moon." He has the voice for it. When I was writing it, I envisioned Gregg Allman singing it. I'm always happy to play "Georgia Moon" for people, and Chris always liked it when my band, Coupe de Ville, did it. He asked me if it would be alright for him to cut it, and it became one of the high points of the album. He and I became good buddies. He also played on my *Red Hot* solo album. The Marshall Tucker band has been his home for several years now, but occasionally we get to play gigs together, some duos and a few gigs with other musicians. We've played the Big House and several venues. Chris is an exciting performer, and he brought a new life to the Marshall Tucker Band.

Another outstanding artist is E.G. Kight, "the Georgia Songbird." Her full name is Eugenia Gail Kight. She started out going by Gail Kight but thought her name sounded too country even though she was doing country at the time. There were a lot of female singers using initials at the time— K.D. Lang, K.T. Oslin. So, she thought E.G. sounded better than Gail. I call her my little soul sister. She's a wonderful person and just a great singer.

The first record I did on her, back in the 1980s, was country, but soon she switched to blues. I can't get enough of hearing her sing. I recorded her last four or five albums. She's one of my set of studio singers, my first call. She and Becky Hataway are two I use the most. Becky's a Christian country singer. But their voices just complement each other. Sometimes I have a third singer, Willie Morris, join them. Willie was a member of the band Cameo that had the hit "Word Up." Willie lives here in Macon, and the three of them together have an unusual mix of vocal styles, and it's just wonderful. The three of them also sang on my *Red Hot* CD.

I guess you could say that every time the doorbell rings, I'm wondering if it's another Marshall Tucker Band with another "Heard It in a Love Song." It's about time we had another one of those!

Another guy I really enjoyed working with is Kunio Kishida from Japan. I first met him about fifteen years ago at Johnny Sandlin's sixtieth birthday party. Then he invited me to play on his album, *Alabama Boy* in 2011. Johnny was producing it at Muscle Shoals Sound—the second studio at the armory, not the Jackson Highway building. I also played on his next album, *Slide Angel*, as well. After Johnny passed away, Kunio cut the basic tracks for a new album at Muscadine. He sent the tapes to various other places to add additional musicians. He sent it back to Muscle Shoals, and I think Scott Boyer played on it. That would have been one of Scott's very last sessions. Kunio took it back to Tokyo and added some guitar parts, then he sent it back to me again, and Chuck Leavell and I played on it. Then we sent it back to them to be mixed and mastered, so his album took a little tour around the world! But that's how records are done these days. It's a lot easier to email a file than to round up all the musicians. But Kunio and I became fast friends, just lifelong friends, and his wife and son are among the most honorable people I know, just like he is.

I've always said that I love music but hate the "music business." The longer I stay in this business, the less I think I understand it. Now, there seem to be fewer major record companies, and they will cut you from the label unless you sell millions of records. There was a time when a label like Warner Bros. would keep a band around just for the sake of art. Look at Little Feat. I don't think they ever sold millions of records in their heyday, but their fans were loyal and so was the label.

I don't understand labels run on computer sites, but that's where most of the music is being sold. I miss the old days of going to a record store and physically picking up an LP, reading the back cover—actually *holding* something in your hands. I don't get that feeling from computer downloads. And the genie is out of the bottle; once you've downloaded it, people can copy it over and over, and the musician doesn't get a dime for their invested time and sacrifices.

Around 1989 I had a band called Coupe de Ville that lasted for about three years. We mostly played local clubs and was more a labor of love than a labor of financial return. We just picked out songs that we loved. We did a Delaney & Bonnie version of Dave Mason's "Only You Know and I Know." We did Bobby Whitlock's "Why Does Love Have to Be So Sad?" We just did our own take on these songs even though most people thought they were original tunes. Coupe de Ville was all local guys—Bruce Whitten was the lead singer and guitar player; Dallas Moore was the other guitar player. We had a couple of different bass players. Eric Wynn played bass, and then James Mills came in to play. George Hall was on drums, and I played keyboards. This band ended in 1992, but if you look me up on the internet it still says "Paul Hornsby has his own band called Coupe de Ville."

12

Reunion:
The Capricorn Reunion
Rhythm Section

The Rhythm Section dates back to right after Hour Glass broke up. Jerry Wexler discovered Duane Allman when Duane was doing session work in Muscle Shoals, Alabama. Wexler told Phil Walden about Allman, and he signed Duane to his new record label. One of the earliest visions Walden had for his new record company was a rhythm section in the image of Stax and Muscle Shoals Sound. Over the years, Johnny Sandlin and I had assembled a pool of musicians that we used as side men for our acts.

The whole Capricorn Rhythm Section reunion happened quite by accident. Around 2006, Johnny Sandlin was involved with the 2nd Street Music Hall, which Carl Weaver had started in Gadsden, Alabama. Weaver had a studio built in there to record bands live, and he started a record label called Rockin' Camel. Scott Boyer, Tommy Talton, Bill Stewart, and I got together to perform and to celebrate Johnny's sixtieth birthday. Then Lee Roy Parnell came in as our special guest. I don't think we even rehearsed; we just looked at it as a party. There were a lot of other bands that played too. But this combination worked well. We were on-stage, looking at each other and thinking, "We need to do this again!" So, we decided we might start playing some gigs. We didn't know what format we were going to use, but I remember that Bill Stewart showed up at the first rehearsal with one of those little plywood boxes they use for a drum. We figured we'd just do an acoustic version of the band, but we quickly decided we were going to have to have drums and go electric. The Capricorn Rhythm Section ended up being Bill Stewart, Scott Boyer, Tommy Talton, Johnny Sandlin, and myself.

It was like riding a bicycle the first time we all got back together. It just fell together. We were playing different songs we had been involved in, from tunes by Cowboy, from Gregg's *Laid Back*, Eddie Hinton, Marshall Tucker, and Dickey Betts. We were also doing newer stuff like Boyer's "Don't Hit Me No More" and "She Cranks My Tractor." We did Tommy's "Watch Out Baby," and played several gigs, including the Skydog fest and several other shows at 2nd Street Music Hall in Gadsden where the live album (*Alive at Second Street Music Hall*) was recorded.

The Georgia Music Hall of Fame was happening in Macon at the time, and they asked me to come and play their Alive at Five concert one Tuesday. I said "Wait a minute! I'm not a singer. I've never sung live in my life." At that point, I had not recorded *Red Hot*, so I didn't do solo shows. The girl was disappointed and asked, "Does that mean you won't do it?" That was right as we were regrouping the Capricorn Rhythm Section, so I told her I'd ask them about playing.

We were setting up to play. Lee Roy was there, and Scott or Tommy invited Gregg Allman, and he came. I was nervous and afraid nobody was going to show up. There wasn't any publicity—it was mostly word of mouth, really. We set up and got a sound check, then we were going to go home, eat supper, and change clothes. Somebody asked me if I had looked outside. I didn't know what they meant, but, when I looked, the line of people waiting to get in stretched around the building. I didn't take the time to go home or anything. The place was packed. There were so many people that some had to stand out in the lobby and watch the show on closed circuit TV. I was surprised, but that was our beginning. We had that band for a year or two. We'd have different guest stars with us, Bonnie Bramlett, Jimmy Hall, or Lee Roy Parnell. Of course, it soon became a business and wasn't as much fun anymore. We just kind of dropped it. But I was quite proud of the live album we did.

As time has passed, so has the chance of playing together again. We lost Gregg Allman on May 27, 2017, then Johnny Sandlin on September 19, 2017, and Scott Boyer on February 13, 2018. It's all just happy memories now, but we sure had some fun.

13

Indians

One of my main hobbies is Native American culture and primitive skills. It goes back to my youth, living on a farm, running through the woods, swinging on vines. I tried to sound like Tarzan, which sounds funny coming out of a nine-year-old. But jungle living always appealed to me. As an adult, I got pretty good at some of the primitive skills, and later was teaching classes at the Ocmulgee National Monument, Fort Hawkins, some of the museums here and there, along with a couple of festivals up in Maryland. I taught how to start a fire with friction and how to make weaponry. My specialty, though, is making arrows like the Southeastern Indians did, using all natural materials, nothing purchased. I use wild turkey feathers and make my stone points to go on them. I get a thrill out of that.

I also do trap-building and wild plant identification—plants you can eat, plants you can take for medicinal purposes. I teach folks about *atlatls*. That was a spear about six feet long. Lots of folks find what they think are arrowheads, but they are two to three inches long. There's no way you could put something that big that on an arrow. Those are atlatl heads. In other cultures of the world, atlatls were used long before the advent of bows and arrows. Australians, for example, never used bows and arrows, but atlatls are still used there today. Bows and arrows were only invented here about fifteen hundred years ago. When you think of the whole span of time, that's a blink of an eye.

Early man hunted mammoths with the atlatl. They would go out hunting, maybe five or ten hunters, surround the mammoth on all sides, and hurl the atlatls darts at it. (They were six feet long, but they called them atlatl "darts.") Those weapons were used for 40,000 years, and mammoths were hunted to extinction this way.

As a kid, I was an avid comic book reader—not super-heroes, but cowboys and Indians. Even before I could read, I could tell what was going on by looking at the pictures. I'd see these points on the arrows, and I had no idea what they were made of. So, I got my daddy's tin snips and some tops off cans. I'd cut triangular shapes from them and tie them on. I made some of the most crooked arrows a seven-year-old ever had. My daddy would see me with my hands all sliced up from cutting them on the cans, and he'd get onto me. One day, he said, "Boy, the Indians didn't make arrowheads out of tin cans, they made 'em out of stone." I thought there was no way you'd tie a rock to the end of an arrow. He took me to a field he'd discovered where we could find some arrow points. I think we found about ten that afternoon. The field was just loaded with them. There was something just magical about that experience, and that afternoon changed my whole life. The only other thing that ever made me feel that way was music. When it came time to go to college, I learned that I'd have to major in anthropology since archeology is a branch of anthropology. Then I found out how much school was involved for that career—I'd have to probably go to school for ten years. I wanted to dig up stuff like Indiana Jones. Back then, the primary option for an archeologist was to become a teacher, a college professor. So, I got discouraged before I could even get started, and I majored in rock and roll music instead. But I continued looking for arrowheads and studying the Indians and became friends with many Indians. I still call them Indians, and all the ones I know prefer that name. They were called Indians for a long time; some prefer that name, and some prefer to be called Native American, Indigenous, or by their tribal affiliation.

I have studied and read countless books, and now I'm one of a very few in Macon who can speak the Creek Indian language. The Creek history runs hand in hand with Georgia history. During most of Georgia's colonial period, the Creeks outnumbered European colonists as well as enslaved Africans. By the 1760s, they had become a minority. There is a wealth of books available on the Creeks, and anyone so inclined could spend hours reading the history online.

I learned skills such as arrow and spear construction, trap building, and fire starting—everything they do on that show *Naked and Afraid*, except I don't get naked. Be thankful for that. I've done a traditional sweat lodge with the Seminoles in Florida. I remember sitting in the sweat lodge with some nude Seminole women and thinking, "If the guys back home could only see me now!" It was so, so hot in there that

I could hardly breathe. I had to pull the covers up from the ground and stick my nose out just to breathe. But it was very relaxing and healing.

I do primitive skills exhibitions every now and then, where I display all my arrows, atlatls, and spears. I toss a few of them, shoot a few of them, and start some fires from scratch—anything anybody wants to know about.

14

Cowboys

The cowboys in my comic books interested me as much as the Indians. I always played the Indian, but I loved cowboys too. Today, I have over a hundred channels on my TV, but there's never anything on. I watch the old Westerns. I start off the evening with *Wagon Train*. And I sometimes watch *Rawhide*, mostly because of Clint Eastwood's character, Rowdy Yates. I wasn't crazy about that show, but Eastwood stood out. I loved his character "the Man with No Name" from *The Good, the Bad and the Ugly*, *Fistful of Dollars*, and *For a Few Dollars More*. They called them Spaghetti Westerns because they had an Italian director, but I think they were filmed in Spain. They had been out for a few years before being sold to American distributors as a package deal for all three. Americans ate them up.

As a boy, my dad watched a lot of singing cowboy movies, and he'd play a lot of those old songs on his guitar. Then I got hooked on them, especially Roy Rogers and Gene Autry. Then I heard the Sons of the Pioneers and grew to love them. I still do to this day.

On Saturdays, if I started begging early enough in the day, I could wear my daddy down and he might take me to the movies. He took me to the drive-in more than the regular theater because it was cheaper. He had to buy me a ticket for the theater, but I was so little that they let me in the drive-in for free. We'd go to see those cowboys, some singing, some not, and we'd talk about how big those cowboys were on the screen. I'd ask my daddy why those cowboys were so big, and he explained that they had to blow the image up to fit the screen. For some reason, I just couldn't figure that out.

My mother sometimes went with us to the Westerns, and I remember her saying, "That's the same rock they were hiding behind last Saturday night!" It made me mad that she was making fun of it, but she was right—they shot at the same places over and over. Out closer to Los Angeles were the Vasquez Rocks. It's on my "to do" list the next time I go to California to visit some of those shooting sites. Long Pine was one of those places; all the Hopalong Cassidy movies were shot at Long Pine.

My Daddy was a true child of the Depression. I kidded him the rest of his life about being a tight wad. He could pinch a penny like nobody I'd ever seen. When we'd go to the movies, they'd run those cartoon ads for hotdogs and sodas at the concession stand before they'd play the movie. Man, they made them look so good. All these teenagers would be getting out of their cars and heading to the concession stand. I'd start telling my daddy I needed a Pepsi. I was thirsty. I remember him reaching back over the seat and pulling out a hot Pepsi Cola. He'd have a whole carton of hot drinks. I told him the ones in the concession stand were so much better, but he'd argue that these were the same thing. I used to kid him about that. I made him so mad.

I also collect old movies. Not just videos, but full-sized film rolls. Around 1979 I started collecting 16mm films. I've got every movie Gene Autry or Roy Rogers ever did. The ones that are really sought after are the uncut versions. Originally those movies ran seventy to seventy-five minutes, but when they showed them on TV back in the '50s, they would cut them down to fifty-four minutes and leave six minutes for commercials. After they cut them down, they'd often throw the "extra" away—even the negative. It became hard to find one that was uncut, but that's what I was always striving for because the part they cut out was usually the songs. We used to have people over and project the movies outside against the side of the house. I sewed a couple of sheets together and put some eyehooks in them and hung them on the outside of the house. We'd invite neighbors over, and we'd all sit out there and watch cowboy movies. There were a few little kids from the neighborhood, and I remember one little girl, no more than six years old, who came over with her parents asking to see a Roy Rogers movie. I told her, "Honey, I bet you are the only person under forty years old in Bibb County who even knows who Roy Rogers is!" But we'd sit out there and watch movies and slap skeeters all night. It was just like being at the drive-in. My neighborhood at the time was filled with widows and divorced people, so the movies fit right in with their lifestyle. They all just loved getting together.

The movies nights ended, though, when a bunch of these neighbor women got dogs. There were about two or three dogs per household. I lived right in the middle, and I didn't have a dog. Well, a dog won't crap in its own yard. They need virgin grass to crap in. All these neighbors' dogs started coming over and crapping in my yard at least twice a day, and we got up in arms about that. We all got angry with one another—and some of them still are—but that broke up our movie night get-togethers. I quit showing the movies. It's sad, because you can't even find a Roy Rogers movie on TV anymore.

For a long time, there were western film conventions. The biggest one was in Charlotte. We'd all go and swap movies and stories, and a lot of times some of the stars from the old movies would come to mingle with the fans. There were rooms where they were always showing films, and a big area with dealers selling movies. It was great. Very few if any of those stars are still living, and even the fans have pretty much died out. You know the hobby is dead when both the stars and their fans are dead. I still have all my movies, though. I have quite a collection that I keep locked up. I'm very nostalgic about it.

15

Red Hot

Pearl Harbor Day, December 7, 1941, will always be re-
membered by people of our generation as the day that Japan
attacked the United States, but that date took on a much
happier meaning for me in 2009 when I got a phone call
from David Johnson at the Alabama Music Hall of Fame.
He asked me what I was doing on March 25. I told him he
had caught me off guard, and I had no idea what I would be
doing in March. He told me to circle that date on my calen-
dar because I was being inducted into the Alabama Music
Hall of Fame. I went right through the roof. I was truly not
expecting it. I thought that since I did most of my work in
Georgia, I might someday be inducted into their Hall of
Fame, but Alabama—my home state—was a huge surprise.
On March 25, 2010, I was inducted in a ceremony in Mont-
gomery (now it's in Muscle Shoals). It was exciting because
my kids and my mother were there. My dad had passed away
several years prior to that.

I sometimes go over to visit the Hall of Fame, and they'll
have some young girl working in there. I'll say, "I'm Paul
Hornsby, and I came to visit my shirt." Because they have

one of my hippie shirts from the Hour Glass on display in there. I'm proud to be in there; it's a world-class setup. I thought I might get into the Georgia Music Hall of Fame someday, but unfortunately it folded. I don't know if they'll ever reopen, but I hope so.

About a year before I cut *Red Hot*, I was invited to headline a blues festival down in Dothan. There's a DJ down there, Gil Anthony, who does a couple of radio shows called *Blues Power*—one of them in Dothan, the other in Enterprise. He interviewed me on the radio, and we got to talking and became friends, so he had me down for a couple more interviews. He got behind the city of Dothan, which is known as the "mural city," to put my portrait on a wall there. All these old buildings are painted with murals of symbols from Dothan's past, like a wagon hauling cotton, people picking cotton, Spanish explorers, and Indian chiefs. One building has a picture of Johnny Mac Brown, the cowboy star. There are buildings that depict the music stars from that area, not just Dothan, but from what they call the Wire Grass area. Two of the buildings are filled with portraits of musicians like Ray Charles and the Atlanta Rhythm Section. Those walls were full before they got to me, but I ended up on a wall with Hank Williams.

They had an unveiling on May 1, 2010, and I had to go down and give a little speech. I had to hurry back to New Brockton by noon because they had organized a Paul Hornsby Day in my hometown. They had a banner and a barbeque, and that night they had a banquet at the armory hall. Chris Hicks came over and joined a band from Albany,

Georgia, called the Dead Gamblers, and we played music. They had some of my old bandmates from the Pacers, and it was like a Ralph Edwards's *This is Your Life* episode. Some came from as far as Virginia, one from Sarasota, another from Tuscaloosa. I call those three things my Alabama tour. The mayor, Lenwood Herron, and Gil Anthony put the New Brockton thing together. All in all, 2010 was a very special year.

Sharon McConnell-Dickerson is a blind artist who, among other work, creates plaster casts of musicians' hands. She did Johnny Winter's hands two weeks before he died. The night before the festival, there was a show at the Dothan Arts Center, and she had a display of all these musicians' hands. These casts were so detailed, you could see every pimple, every crease, and even the pores in the skin. So, she asked to do mine, and the next day she displayed them. It was kind of creepy, to be honest, like looking at a dead man because they were so realistic. I set her up with Chuck Leavell, and she did his too. She said that she was going to have a display at the Smithsonian that would have all these hands coming up out of the ground and call it "the roots of rock and roll."

In 2015, Gil Anthony called me up again, asking me to headline the Wiregrass Blues Festival in Dothan. I told him the same thing I told the Hall of Fame: "I'm not a singer. I'm just a piano player. I play behind other singers." He wouldn't take no for an answer, so I agreed. There were about three or four months until the festival, so I thought if I could just get three or four songs down, I'd be okay. I got E.G. Kight's band to back me up. We got her on the show, and I figured I'd let her do most of the show. Well, I ended up with enough songs to do a set, and that was the beginning of the *Red Hot* material. A bunch of blues acts played, and they had us play last as the headliner. We kicked into "Mess Around," and everybody got up and started moving toward the stage. I was looking really closely to be sure they were smiling. E.G. sang "Can't You See," and we did a bunch of songs that I had something to do with, and by the end we had a bunch of people on the stage. It went over so well— and I had put so much time into learning the songs—that I thought it would be a shame not to do anything else with them. I decided to cut a CD, so I spent another year researching and practicing. That's how I ended up cutting my first album on myself. I don't know if I'll ever cut another one, but I got the one done! It actually made it into the Americana charts.

There were many people I had worked with over the years I wanted to include on the album, so I ended up with quite a lot of artists—Chuck Leavell, Tommy Talton, Charlie Hayward, Lee Roy Parnell, Bill Stewart, Jack Pearson, E.G. Kight's band, and others.

I took the reverse process in recording this time out. Instead of cutting the music tracks and then adding my keyboard parts last, as I had always done when recording other artists, I decided to cut with piano and drums first. Everything else was added later. That way, the bass parts followed my left hand on the piano. That left hand is the important thing on the kind of music on this CD. It took about two years from start to finish.

It's a new day now, especially regarding Southern rock. Music always changes with each new crop of musicians. Even some of the ones who grew up with Southern rock roots might not want to admit it. Southern rock as a genre is probably bigger in Europe today than here. Some Southern bands cut CDs more for European sales than for American. As a result, it's harder to use success as a Southern rock producer as a calling card with today's music, but we ain't planning on stopping anytime soon.

Right now there are a few younger bands like Blackberry Smoke and Marcus King who I like a lot. They are bringing new life to the genre.

Epilogue

I've been extremely fortunate to have been in the company of such talented players and performers throughout my career. However, there is one important person that some might not be aware of.

Near the beginning of this story, I met a beautiful young lady named Jeanne. She had caught my eye and became my biggest fan. Every time I played on stage, I played directly to her. Not long after, she became Mrs. Paul Hornsby, and we were together for the next twenty years. She remained a fan and through the years never failed in her support for my career and the music I was involved in. It was because of her support that I continued in this difficult business of music. Besides being the mother of my two oldest children, April and Jesse, she added her contribution to all the music I participated in. My son Lee would come along later. Though we lived apart for the last several years of her life, she was my constant counsel and had been the song in my life. We lost her suddenly on November 9, 2000. It is to her memory that I dedicate this story.

Jeanne Lowry Hornsby
1944–2000

Afterword

Recording with Paul Hornsby:
A Dream Come True

Anyone who says dreams can't come true is a dumbass. All the way back in 1973 I began my obsession with the music and bands that came out of Capricorn Records in the small town of Macon, Georgia. I have told the story countless times, but it does indeed go back to one late-night television broadcast called "Saturday Night in Macon, Georgia." It was a special edition of the music variety show *Don Kirshner's Rock Concert*. In those days, I never missed ABC-TV's *In Concert*, NBC's *Midnight Special* or *Kirshner's Rock Concert*. My Friday and Saturday nights were spent on the sofa, eating bologna and cheese sandwiches, drinking a Coke, and grooving to the live bands.

On this particular evening, I was caught off guard. A friend at school had loaned me his Allman Brothers *At Fillmore East* double album, and I had been simply blown away by the sound. Around the same time, I had managed to get my underage butt into a club in Spartanburg, South Carolina, called Uncle Sam's, where I sat in awe of the guitar player in a band called Toy Factory. The guitarist was Toy Caldwell, and the band was mere months away from fame as the Marshall Tucker Band.

Some young girl was on my TV, speaking with the most pronounced Southern drawl, talking about Macon, Georgia, and how it was becoming a hot bed for great new rock groups. Just before she spoke, there was a short clip of the Allman Brothers, their crew, and their family seated on a porch on some old country home. The camera closed in on Gregg Allman as he said, "Welcome to Macon, Georgia." I sat transfixed for the next ninety minutes, watching this red-hot band called Wet Willie performing on an outdoor stage and just rocking like nobody's business. Then the cameras moved inside the Macon Opera House for a smoking set by the Marshall Tucker Band and a great set from the Allman Brothers Band. My life changed that night.

I began buying albums by the Allman Brothers and Wet Willie, and, of course, Tucker's debut. All of us in Spartanburg were thrilled for our hometown boys. They were on their way. I started buying more Capricorn records by Cowboy, Grinderswitch, and many others. I'd study the liner notes like a detective. I wanted to know about the people behind the music. A great band needs great managers, producers and engineers. I noticed that every release had one of two men listed as producer: Johnny Sandlin or Paul Hornsby. Johnny Sandlin did most of the Allman stuff, and Paul Hornsby produced all of Marshall Tucker's classic albums, *Fire on the Mountain* (another favorite) by the Charlie

Daniels Band, a couple of platters by Wet Willie, the excellent Eric Quincy Tate, and many others. I became a die-hard fan of Hornsby, even before I knew his earlier history.

After I bought a Panasonic cassette player and a bunch of tapes from a guy who needed money for weed, I listened to several of his tapes, including both volumes of the *Duane Allman Anthology*. That's when I first learned about the band the Hour Glass, a pre-Allman band that featured Gregg and Duane Allman, Johnny Sandlin, and Pete Carr, along with Paul Hornsby. I had no way of knowing that my future would find the great Pete Carr playing on two of my own albums (not to mention my good fortune of singing a duet with the fabulous Capricorn artist Bonnie Bramlett) and having both George McCorkle of Marshall Tucker and Tommy Crain from the Charlie Daniels Band on my records. Of course, the thrill of all thrills came about in 2018, when I recorded an album called *Makin' It Back to Macon* produced by the legendary Paul Hornsby at Muscadine Studios in Macon.

God only knows how many dreams I had over the years of working with Paul one day. I still pinch myself to be sure I'm not dreaming. Recording with Paul was like butter. He is so easygoing and non-demanding. He hears the music in his head a certain way, and as long as you play it that way, you'll be okay. If not, he will do whatever it takes to pull your very best out of you.

I just had to not think about all the gold and platinum records he has produced, or the fact that he worked closely with my true musical heroes. I just set that baggage aside and went with the flow. It was a bonus that Paul agreed to play keys on some of my songs. On one song, he played an old electric Wurlitzer piano. Then he made a simple statement that blew my mind: "That piano belonged to Gregg Allman. He played it on the *Fillmore* album." *What?* I quickly had to regroup; I could not afford to go all "fanboy" on Paul.

During one of the sessions, Paul sat at a piano and started playing and singing to warm up. He did the old song "Hallelujah, I Love Her So," and his piano was amazing, very reminiscent of Dr. John's New Orleans style.

This album had been over ten years in the making—well, not the actual making, but the planning. My last album, *Something Heavy*, was recorded and released in 2005. For those keeping score at home, that's thirteen years ago. As far back as 2008 I was planning to do a new record, but as they say, "life got in the way." I had written the title track, mostly, and I had a vision of the album being produced by the great Paul Hornsby. I didn't even know Paul at the time. I had interviewed him for my *Gritz* magazine, but it would be several more years and a couple more interviews before I started feeling like he was my friend. Now I am working with him on his biography. How cool is that? I knew I wanted him to produce, but I had no idea how I could make it happen.

I also dreamed of asking some of the old Capricorn and other Southern Rock artists to do guest spots on *Makin' It Back to Macon*. The first one I wanted to ask was founding Cowboy member (and one of my favorite singer-songwriter-guitarists) Tommy Talton. After one of his gigs at the Melting Point in Athens in about 2008, I just came out and asked him. I even told him about the blues song and my idea of just having him play some old-school Robert Johnson type slide and me singing, maybe one of us stomping a foot. To my surprise, he agreed.

I was blessed with other fine musicians for the sessions, including my longtime band mate from the Buffalo Hut Coalition, Greg Yeary, a great guitarist who also wrote one of the songs and co-wrote another; Joey Parrish and Daniel Jackson of the Silver Travis Band; and Towson "Lefty" Engsberg on drums, who is a member of the late Tommy Crain's band the Crosstown Allstars (the band kept playing after Tommy's death); Austin, Texas, honky-tonker Billy Eli (who recently co-produced my EP *The Austin Sessions*); and the magnificent Georgia songbird herself, E.G. Kight, on backing vocals. Add to that the magical piano work of my producer Paul Hornsby, and we had quite a nice group of players.

The recording sessions were spread out over a month. There were probably five in all. The first day it was Paul, Towson Engsberg, and I. Towson tracked the drums, and I played acoustic guitar. The bass player I planned to use, Joey, couldn't get off work, so we were stuck at the studio with no bassist. Billy Eli was in from Austin to add some guitar, and through his connections, we found Hal Branstetter, who came in to play bass on the song "Makin' it Back to Macon."

Another day we spent with Tommy Talton playing guitar, slide and Dobro on several songs. Again, I couldn't overthink it. I just watched and listened as be played Dobro on "Smell All the Roses," and slide guitar on the title track and others. Just amazing.

I have known Greg Yeary since college. He and I had a band called the Buffalo Hut Coalition in the 1980s, and the guy is an amazing guitarist. He also wrote the song "Like Water" on the album and co-wrote with me "My Baby Drives a Mercedes Benz." He and his wife, Connie, came down from Carolina for a day, and we knocked out his parts. Greg is the bomb.

Another session found me returning to Macon, accompanied by Joey Parrish and Daniel Jackson of the Silver Travis band. Joey added bass to a few songs, and Daniel played some great flat picking guitar on "Both Feet on the Ground" and "Woman in the Moon." He also added some killer harmony vocals.

My friend Billy Bob Thornton of the Boxmasters (as well as movies and TV) added my prologue and epilogue spoken-word segments to the album, and Paul did a brilliant (as always) mix.

As an interesting aside, the cover photo for the album features my stepdaughter, Hannah Greene, and my first grandchild, Zoe. When I began planning the album in 2008, I had thought about the cover. My late wife, Jill McLane, was a talented photographer and had shot the cover photos for three of my previous albums as well as hundreds of photos to accompany articles I had written for magazines. In 2008, she took Hannah and Zoe to a backroad location and shot a series of photos with her digital camera. Several months ago, I had the startling realization that I didn't have any idea where those photo files were. I remember backing them up a few different ways, including on CD, but no matter how hard I looked, I couldn't find them. I gave up and planned to reshoot with another model. We were more than halfway finished with the recording when a random search of my computer for something completely unrelated lead me to a folder marked with a date in 2008. That's all. I opened it to find all the Hannah [and Zoe] photos. Some call it luck. I call it a blessing.

While *Makin' It Back to Macon* fulfilled many of my dreams, others didn't happen. I had asked my buddy Jakson Spires (Blackfoot) about playing drums on a song or two. He was all in, but he passed away. I also had commitments from Marshall Tucker Band guitarist George McCorkle (who played on my previous album) as well as two members of Grinderswitch, Dru Lombar and Larry Howard, all of whom we lost too early. Despite these losses, I was honored to have so many talented musicians contribute to the album. While I brought the songs to the table, the recording was a group effort. Everyone contributed ideas, but we all deferred to Paul Hornsby for the final decisions…as it should be.

Watching Paul work was a true highlight of my life. He's just so good at it, with not a drop of ego to cloud the proceedings. My dreams had come true. Sometimes all you have to do is believe.

—*Michael Buffalo Smith*

Appendix: Discography

Artist	Title	Label, Year	Highest Chart	Awards
Sundown	*Sundown*	Ampex, 1970		
Eric Quincey Tate	*Drinking Man's Friend*	Capricorn, 1972		
Marshall Tucker Band	*Marshall Tucker Band*	Capricorn, 1973	#29	Gold record
	"Take the Highway"	Capricorn, 1973		
	"Can't You See"	rel. 1973, 1977	#75	
Marshall Tucker Band	*A New Life*	Capricorn, 1974	#37	Gold record
Marshall Tucker Band	*Where We All Belong*	Capricorn, 1974	#54	Gold record
	"This Ol' Cowboy"	Capricorn, 1974		
Marshall Tucker Band	*Searchin' for a Rainbow*	Capricorn, 1975	#15	Gold record
	"Fire on the Mountain"	Capricorn, 1975	#38	
	"Searchin' for a Rainbow"	Capricorn, 1975	#15	Gold record
Marshall Tucker Band	*Long Hard Ride*	Capricorn, 1976	#32	

	"Long Hard Ride"	Capricorn, 1977	#32	Grammy-nom
Marshall Tucker Band	*Carolina Dreams*	Capricorn, 1977	#23	Platinum award
	"Heard It in a Love Song"	Capricorn, 1977	#10	
Marshall Tucker Band	*Stompin' Room Only*	Shout! Factory, 2003		
Charlie Daniels Band	*Fire on the Mountain*	Kama Sutra, 1974	#38	Platinum record
		Re-release, Epic Records		
	"The South's Gonna Do It Again"	Kama Sutra, 1974	#29	
	"Long Haired Country Boy"	Kama Sutra, 1975	#56	
Charlie Daniels Band	*Saddle Tramp*	Epic, 1976	#7	Gold record
Charlie Daniels Band	*High Lonesome*	Epic, 1976	#17	
Charlie Daniels Band	*Midnight Wind*	Epic, 1977	#42	
Wet Willie Band	*The Wetter the Better*	Capricorn, 1976	#133	Gold record
Wet Willie Band	*Left Coast Live*	Capricorn, 1977	#191	

Kitty Wells	*Forever Young*	Capricorn, 1975
Grinderswitch	*Honest to Goodness*	Capricorn, 1974
Grinderswitch	*Macon Tracks*	Capricorn, 1975
Grinderswitch	*Pullin' Together*	Capricorn, 1976
Grinderswitch	*Red Wing*	Atco., 1977
Marshall Tucker Band, Bonnie Bramlett, Grinderswitch	*Hotels, Motels and Road Shows*	Capricorn, 1978
Marshall Tucker Band, Charlie Daniels Band	*South's Greatest Hits Vol. I*	Capricorn, 1977
Marshall Tucker Band, Charlie Daniels Band, Wet Willie Band	*South's Greatest Hits Vol. II*	Capricorn, 1978
Various	*Volunteer Jam*	Capricorn, 1976
Various	*Volunteer Jam Vol. III & IV*	Epic, 1978

Bobby Whitlock	*Rock Your Sox Off*	Capricorn, 1976
Target	*Captured*	A&M, 1977
Randy Richards	*Randy Richards*	A&M, 1978
Good Brothers	*Doin' the Wrong Things Right*	RCA, 1978
Good Brothers	*Some Kind of Woman*	RCA, 1979
Heartwood	*Nothin' Fancy*	GRC, 1975
Two Guns	*Balls Out*	Capricorn, 1979
Cooder Brown	*Cooder Brown*	Lone Star, 1978
Missouri	*Welcome to Missouri*	Polydor, 1979
Marcia Waldorf	*Memoranda*	Capricorn, 1975
Randy Howard	*All–American Redneck*	Warner/Viva, 1983
Chris Hicks	*Funky Broadway*	Walden Records, 1998
Various	*Urban Cowboy Soundtrack Vol. II*	Epic, 1980
Normal Town Flyers	*Play Something I Like*	Mad Dog, 1982
Sugar Creek Band	*Sugar Creek Band*	Muscadine, 1985

Potliquor "New York City You Ain't" Capricorn, 1976

Jim Beer & The River *Turtle Island* Sunshine, 1995

E.G. Kight *Lip Service* 2011
Co-produced with E.G. Kight

E.G. Kight *A New Day* 2014
Co-produced with E.G. Kight

Lisa Biales *Just Like Honey*
Co-produced with E.G. Kight

Lisa Biales *Belle of the Blues*
Co-produced with E.G. Kight

Michael Buffalo Smith *Makin' It Back to Macon* Dreaming Buffalo, 2018

Selected Reading

Freeman, Scott. *Midnight Riders*. Boston: Little Brown, 1995.

Leavell, Chuck. *Between Rock and a Home Place*. Macon: Mercer University Press, 2004.

Sandlin, Anathalee G. *A Never-Ending Groove: Johnny Sandlin's Musical Odyssey*. Music and the American South. Macon: Mercer University Press, 2012.

Smith, Michael Buffalo. *Capricorn Rising: Conversations in Southern Rock*. Music and the American South. Macon: Mercer University Press, 2017.

Smith, Michael Buffalo. *Rebel Yell: An Oral History of Southern Rock*. Macon: Mercer University Press, 2015.

Special Thanks

To my father, Edd Hornsby, who taught me my first three guitar chords and how to play *Wildwood Flower*. I was on my way.

To Lorenzo Downing, the first professional musician I ever knew. He was very generous with his time and taught me how to play "Honky Tonk" and "What'd I Say?" I was starting to feel the magic in what music had in store.

To Cliff Hurter, owner of Tuscaloosa Music Service, who gave me a paying job that still involved music, teaching guitar lessons. First time in a few years that I wasn't skinny.

To Duane Allman, guitar legend, who taught me that just when you are beginning to think you're good, you have a lot left to learn.

To Phil Walden, president of Capricorn Records, for believing.

To the Marshall Tucker Band, Charlie Daniels Band, Wet Willie Band, and others who gave me a producing career.

To Michael Buffalo Smith, for his love of the kind of music that I play and wanting to write about it.

To John Charles Griffin for help with copy editing and proofreading.

—PH

Thanks to Paul Hornsby, Phil Walden, and Frank Fenter of Capricorn, Dr. Marc Jolley, Marsha Luttrell, Mary Beth Kosowski, Robin Duner Fenter, Hal Stewart, Laura and Steve Flacy, Joey Parrish, Timothy Shook, Scott Greene, my team of doctors, including Lori Malvern, as well as my supportive friends.

—*MBS*

About the Authors

Paul Hornsby is a former member of the music groups The Minutes and later Hour Glass, with bandmates Duane Allman, Gregg Allman, Johnny Sandlin, and Pete Carr. In the 1970s, he was a producer and engineer at the legendary Capricorn Records. A 2010 inductee of the Alabama Music Hall of Fame, he has produced several artists including the Marshall Tucker Band, the Charlie Daniels Band, Wet Willie, Kitty Wells, and Bobby Whitlock. Currently, he is owner/engineer at Muscadine Recording Studio in Macon, Georgia.

Michael Buffalo Smith was born in Spartanburg, South Carolina, and lived in various bungalows on the east coast before returning to his hometown in 2014. Smith has been a contributor to various magazines including *Rolling Stone, Goldmine,* and *Mojo* and has authored eleven books. He is also a performing songwriter and editor of the online magazine KUDZOO.

Index

"Alabama Boy" 127
Allmanac 40
Allman Brothers Band 31, 42, 45, 51, 53, 64, 82, 83, 87, 91, 97, 98, 111, 146, 147
Allman, Duane 26, 39, 42-44, 50, 51, 54, 56, 57, 59-61, 64, 70-72, 129, 148
Allman, Gregg 26, 39, 41-44, 48, 50-52, 64, 71, 72, 77, 98, 131, 147, 149
Allman Joys, The 23, 26, 33, 39, 41, 54, 55
"A New Life" 88
Anthony, Gil 142
Armstrong, Tippy 58
Asleep at the Wheel 106
"At Fillmore East" 146
Atkins, Chet 12, 36
Atlatl 132, 133
Autry, Gene 136, 138
Baines, Barbara 49
Ballenger, Paul 26, 30, 31
Bangs, Lester 75, 83
Barons, The 20, 21
Beatles, The 32, 51
Beavers, Chuck. 19
Beer, Jim & The Rivers 117
Benton, Brook 74
Berry, Chuck 21, 30
Betts, Dickey (Richard) 31, 94, 96, 98, 111, 112, 130
Biales, Lisa 17

Big Brother & The Holding Company 46
Bishop, Elvin 94, 99, 107
Bland, Bobby 40
Boogie Chillun 62
Booker, James 27
Booker T. & The MG's 61
Boxmasters, The 151
Boyer, Scott 96, 129, 130, 131
Bramlett, Bonnie 90, 98, 131, 148
Briggs, David 32
Brown, Carolyn 101
Brown, David 96
Brown, James 53
Buffalo Hut Coalition 150, 151
Buffalo Springfield 46
Buffett, Jimmy 69
Burdon, Eric and The Animals 24, 47
Butterfield, Paul 47
Butts, Glen 58
Caldwell, Tommy 82, 91
Caldwell, Toy 80, 82, 84, 90, 91, 92, 96, 113, 147
Campbell, Charlie 26, 30, 31
Campbell Joseph "Red Dog" 65
Cannon, Dyan 116
Cantonwine, David 74
Capricorn Records 57-80

Capricorn Rhythm Section 62, 66, 129-135
Captain Beyond 94
"Captured" 117
Carr, Pete 37, 45, 50, 57, 61, 66, 101, 148
"Carolina Dreams" 90, 91
Carter, Jimmy 70, 79, 107
Carrigan, Jerry 32, 69
Cartwright, Angela 48, 49
Causey, Davis 103
Channel, Bruce 15
Charles, Ray 24, 26, 27
Charlie Daniels Band 58
Cher 121
Collins, Allen 52
Cocker, Joe 99
Commander Cody & His Lost Planet Airmen 89
Como, Perry 32
Connell, Bill 23, 31, 33, 55
Cooder Brown 106
Cooke, Sam 43
Coupe de Ville 126, 128
Cowboy 130, 147, 149
Crain, Tommy 148, 150
Creek Indians 134
Crosstown Allstars, The 150
Crusaders, The 66
Cunningham, Bob 22
Daniels, Charlie 88, 89, 98, 100, 105, 108, 109, 110-118, 147
Derek & The Dominos 78
DiGregorio, Taz 112
Dorsey, Mary 96
Dr. John 26, 27, 45, 65, 72
"Drinking Man's Friend" 74-76

"Duane Allman Anthology" 148
Dudek, Les 78
Dylan, Bob 96
Eastwood, Clint 121, 136
Eli, Billy 150
Engsberg, Towson 150
Eric Quincy Tate 73-76, 148
Eubanks, Jerry 82
Everett, Chad 49
FAME Studios 32
Fenter, Frank 70-72, 76, 77, 103
Fillmore Auditorium 46
"Fire On the Mountain" 105, 109, 110, 112, 147
Five Minutes, The 23-15, 28-28, 40, 93
"Forever Young" 97
Freeman, Scott 77
Frizell & West 121
Garret, Snuff 121
Georgia Music Hall of Fame 141
Gomer Pyle USMC 49
Good Brothers, The 117
Goodson Brothers 15
Graham, Bill 46, 47
Grant's Lounge 74, 81
Grateful Dead 46
Gray, Doug 82
Greene, Hannah Jane 151, 152
Grinderswitch 90, 94, 98, 99, 147
Gunder, John 19
Haas, Johnny 19
Hall, Donna 96
Hall, Jimmy 79, 131

Harris, Jonathan 48
Hawkins, Roger 66
Hayward, Charlie 57, 143
Headren, Tippi 49
Heartwood 103, 105
Helms, Don 10
Hendrix, Jimi 51
Herron, Lenwood 142
Hicks, Chris 89, 117, 125
Hidley, Tom 67
Highland, Mike 71
Hinton, Eddie 30, 31, 35, 37, 57, 130
Hirsch, Rick 79
Hogue, Doug 21
Holmes, Flournoy 111
"Honest to Goodness" 98
Hornsby, Ace 4
Hornsby, Bertie 4
Hornsby, Ed 3, 114
Hornsby, Jeanne Lowry 145
Hornsby, Magdalene 3
"Hotels, Motels & Road Shows" 90
Hour Glass, The 24, 39-56, 57, 60, 88, 93, 129, 141, 148
Howard, Larry 152
Howard, Randy 119-128
Hughey, John 96
Hurter, Cliff 23, 24
Jackson, Daniel 150, 151
Jamison, Jimi 117
Jefferson Airplane 46
Jenkins, Johnny 72
Johanson, Jaimoe 64, 72, 94
Johns, Sammy 103
Johnson, David 140
Johnson, Jimmy 32, 66

Jones, Booker T. 26
Jones, Tom 34
Joplin, Janis 46, 47
Keller, Bob 44, 45
Kent, Richard 58
King, B.B. 30
Kight, E.G. 126, 143, 150
Kirshner, Don 91, 146
Kishida, Kunio 127
Knight, Joyce 96
"Lady's Choice" 99
"Laid Back" 77, 78, 130
Landau, Martin 49
Leavell, Chuck 27, 31, 44, 58, 59, 61, 77, 79, 96, 127, 142, 143
"Left Coast Live" 77
Lennon, John 50
Little Richard 53, 61
Lockhart, June 48
Lombar, Dru 79, 98, 152
Lost in Space 48
Loudermilk, John 36
Lynyrd Skynyrd 111
Mack, Lonnie 33
Maddox, Isaiah 3
Maddox, Stella 3
Mahal, Taj 72
"Makin' it Back to Macon" 148
Marino, George 86
Mark V, The 26
Marshall Tucker Band, The 53, 75, 76, 80, 81-94, 91, 93, 97, 100, 102, 105, 112, 114, 126, 127, 130, 147
Maxey, Zoe 151, 152
McConnell-Dickerson, Sharon 142

McCorkle, George 82, 148, 152
McCormick, Donnie 74
McEuen, Bill 41, 24
McKinney, Mabron "Wolf" 33, 35, 39, 41, 44
McQueen, Steve 73
Mission Impossible 49
Miles, Buddy 47
Miller, Steve 98
Misfitz, The 31
Missouri 106
Mull, Martin 91
Mumy, Bill 49
Nalls, Jimmy 79, 106, 115
Nelson, Willie 106, 116
Nitty Gritty Dirt Band 41
"Nothin' Fancy" 104
Oakley, Berry 30, 58, 59, 60, 72
Offord, Eddie 76
One Percent, The 52
Orbison, Roy 15
Paul Revere & The Raiders 50
Pacers, The 22, 26, 142
Parnell, Lee Roy 129, 131, 131, 143
Parrish, Joey 150, 151
Pearson, Jack 143
Petty, Joe Dan 98
Pfeifer, Diane 96
Penn, Dan 26
Pickett, Wilson 40
Popwell, Robert 61, 66
Potliquor 100
Price, Alan 24
Professor Longhair 27
Putnam, Norbert 32, 69

Redding, Otis 19, 53, 61, 72, 96
"Red Hot" 126, 130, 140-144
Riddle, Paul T. 82, 94
Richards, Randy 114-116
"Rock Your Socks Off" 78
Rockin' Camel Records 129
Rogers, Roy 105, 136, 138
Rossington, Gary 52
"Saddle Tramp" 113
Sandlin, Johnny 29-31, 33, 35, 37, 39, 40, 50, 57, 59-61, 62, 71, 72, 77, 81, 95, 96, 101, 102, 127, 129, 130, 131, 147, 148
Scaggs, Boz 107
"Searchin' for a Rainbow" 94
Silver Travis Band, The 150, 151
Sledge, Percy 64
"Slide Angel" 127
Slim Harpo 19
"Sgt. Pepper's Lonley Hearts Club Band" 51
Smith, Jill McLane 151
Smith, Jimmy 25, 26
"Something Heavy" 149
Spires, Jakson 152
Stein, Andy 89
Stewart, Bill 58, 96, 115, 129, 130, 143
Stills, Stephen 47
"Stompin' Room Only" 90
Sturdevant, John 97
Styles, Fred 21, 26, 30, 33
Sundown 81
Sutton, Frank 49
Survivor 117
Swampers, The 32

INDEX

Talton, Tommy 17, 96, 129, 130, 131, 143, 149
Target 117
Taylor, Alex 73, 76
Taylor, James 68
Taylor, Livingston 65, 73, 101
"The Austin Sessions" 150
"The Marshall Tucker Band" 85
"The Wetter The Better" 77
Thevis, Michael 103
Thomas, Mickey 100
Thomas, Rufas 77
Thornton, Billy Bob 151
Tindol, James 9, 114
"Ton Ton Macoute!" 71
Toy Factory 147
Townsend, John 58
Townsend, Pete 51
Trucks, Butch 64
'Turtle Island" 117
Two Guns 100
University of Alamaba 18
Van Zant, Ronnie 52
Ventures, The 19, 22
Volunteer Jam 108-109
Walden, Phil 60, 61, 62, 68 – 70, 73, 76, 77, 79, 80, 81, 91, 98, 100-103, 105, 107, 129
Webbs, The 15
Wells, Kitty 62, 95
Wet Willie 68, 75, 76, 91, 147, 148
Wexler, Jerry 71, 129
"Where We All Belong" 88, 105
White, Tony Joe 74
White Witch 75

Whiteside, Sam 99
Whitlock, Bobby 78
Williams, Hank 10
Williams, Hank Jr. 80
Wooley, Dick 71
Wright, Johnny 96
Yeary, Greg 150, 151
Young, Neil 47

MUSIC AND THE AMERICAN SOUTH

TITLES IN THE SERIES

Jack and Olivia Solomon, *Honey in the Rock: The Ruby Pickens Tartt Collection of Religious Folk Songs from Sumter County, Alabama*

Zell Miller, *They Heard Georgia Singing*

David Fillingim, *Redneck Liberation: Country Music as Theology*

Willie Perkins, *No Saints, No Saviors: My Years with the Allman Brothers Band*

Anathalee G. Sandlin, *A Never-Ending Groove: Johnny Sandlin's Musical Odyssey*

Michael P. Graves and David Fillingim , ed. *More Than Precious Memories: The Rhetoric Of Southern Gospel Music*

Michael Buffalo Smith, *Prisoner of Southern Rock: A Memoir*, with a Foreword by Billy Bob Thornton

Michael Buffalo Smith, *Rebel Yell: An Oral History of Southern Rock*, with a Foreword by Alan Walden

Willie Perkins and Jack Weston, *The Allman Brothers Band Classic Memorabilia, 1969-1976*, with a Foreword by Galadrielle Allman

Michael Buffalo Smith, *Capricorn Rising: Conversations in Southern Rock*, with a Foreword by Willie Perkins

Michael Buffalo Smith, *From Macon to Jacksonville: More Conversations in Southern Rock*, with a Foreword by Charlie Starr

Michael Buffalo Smith, *The Road Goes on Forever: Fifty Years of The Allman Brothers Band Music (1969–2019)*, with a Foreword Chuck Leavell

Doug Kershaw, *The Ragin' Cajun: Memoir of a Louisiana Man*, with Cathie Pelletier

Don Reid, *The Music of The Statler Brothers: An Anthology*, with a Foreword by Bill and Gloria Gaither

Paul Hornsby, Fix it in the Mix: A Memoir with Michael Buffalo Smith

COMING FALL 2021

Ben Wynne, *Something in the Water: A History of Music in Macon, Georgia, 1823–1980*